SAILING TALL

-

Around the World
on the square-rigged *Passat*
(1946–1948)

-

To all who went and still go to sea to earn a living,
especially those still surviving from the era of sail,
to old shipmates and even "Board-of-Trade acquaintances",
and to all who may have wished to go to sea.

Sailing Tall

Around the World
on the square-rigged *Passat*
(1946–1948)

Max Wood

SEAFARER BOOKS

SHERIDAN HOUSE

© Max Wood 2004

First published in the UK by:
Seafarer Books
102 Redwald Road
Rendlesham
Woodbridge
Suffolk IP12 2TE

2nd impression 2004

And in the USA by:
Sheridan House Inc.
145 Palisade Street
Dobbs Ferry
N.Y. 10522

UK ISBN   0 9542750 2 0
USA ISBN   1 57409 189 1

British Library Cataloguing in Publication Data
Wood, Max
    Sailing tall : around the world on the square-rigged
    Passat, 1946–1948
    1.Wood, Max – Travel 2.Seafaring life – History – 20th
    century 3.Square-riggers 4.Sailors – Great Britain –
    Biography
    I.Title
    910.4 ' 5 ' 092

    ISBN 0954275020

A CIP catalog record for this book is available from the
Library of Congress, Washington, DC

Cover design by Louis Mackay
Typesetting and design by Julie Rainford

Drawings by Max Wood and Boombana Publications
The photographs included in this publication are from Max Wood's
personal archive. They are part of a pool of souvenirs generously
contributed by their shipmates and shoreside friends. The informality
of the process and the time elapsed made it extremely difficult to
determine with absolute certainty the identity of the photographer in
all cases and to renew all contacts at the time of publication. We hope
that no one will be offended if these photographs are not individually
credited. The publisher will honour any reasonable documented claim
for copyright fees.

Printed in Finland by WS Bookwell OY

Contents

PREFACE

The Second World War tolled the death-knell of commercial deep-sea sailing vessels. I had the good fortune to serve at the conclusion of the war, as a young apprentice, aboard one of the few survivors, the *Passat*, in what turned out to be one of the very last voyages of a square-rigged cargo carrier.

To call this event fortunate may well elicit a wry smile in many of my old shipmates. Admittedly, as I shall show in the following pages, the reality of life aboard these old vessels was far removed from the romantic image conveyed by most novels and films. It was gruelling at times.

It was nevertheless exhilarating, and in the days of sail each voyage was a grand adventure of a kind that no modern-day traveller will ever be able to experience.

Looking back on this two-year voyage, I still think that, despite the hardships, I was privileged to go through such a great apprenticeship. Far from turning me away from ships, it equipped me with a wealth of knowledge and experience which enabled me to follow the calling of the sea till retirement forty-six years later.

What partly motivated me to write this story was the realisation that such a powerful formative experience, no longer available to the young men tempted by the sea, was worth recording as a piece of history.

This is also the story of a boy turning into a young man, getting to know the world, maturing and taking his place among his fellow men, coming to terms with the pains and anxieties of leaving behind a troubled family, learning the realities of the love life of seafarers.

This is then in a nutshell the 'full'n by' to 'running free' of the seafaring life on a latter-day square-rigger.

*

By the time of the outbreak of the war, sailing vessels, after plying the oceans from ancient times, could be no further improved in design and construction in their attempt to compete economically with engine-driven ships. The last commercial sailers were not fast clippers but big powerful vessels built to carry as much cargo as possible. They were made of steel, with steel masts and yards and steel wire rope for standing rigging. There were still a few three-mast ones, but most were four-mast barques. This meant square-rigged on the fore, main and mizzen masts, and fore-and-aft on the jigger mast. The last barques in service had, except one or two, centre castles and were known as 'three-island' vessels. They were heavily rigged with 18 square sails, six on each of the fore, main and mizzen masts, plus 16 fore-and-afters, that is, a total of 34 when under full sail. However three of the fore-and-afters were seldom used or even bent.

This then was the type of sailing ships that were still afloat at the end of hostilities in 1945. The sudden end of the war saw world shipping enter a chaotic period. The allied nations returned control of their merchant fleets to their private owners. New tonnage was allocated to shipowners within the Allies to replace tonnage that had been sunk so as to rebuild the companies on a commercial basis and resume full-scale maritime trade as soon as possible. The Axis countries were not for some time allowed any such luxury, in fact they had to hand over a percentage of the meagre tonnage they had left, as reparations, to the victor nations.

Sailing ships in such a situation were a negligible quantity. No one was interested in them at the time with the exception of three German sailing ships, two of which were the last and most modern commercial sailing ships afloat, having only been built, *Priwall* in 1919 and *Padua* in 1926. The former was granted to Chile, the latter to the USSR, and *Kommodore Johnsen*, a somewhat older ship (formerly *Magdalene Vinnen*) also went to the USSR.

Of Finland's sailing ships that survived, *Passat*, *Viking* and *Pommern* were at anchor in Mariehamn, Åland Islands. They too could have been claimed as reparations by allied countries since Finland had been an Axis power until 1944, but maybe none wanted them because the Baltic was then still full of mines. Sailing ships are especially vulnerable in mine-infested waters as they cannot keep to cleared lanes. *Archibald Russel* survived as a war prize in Goole, UK, but then was broken up for scrap. The *Moshulu*, *Abraham Rydberg* and *Winterhude* never sailed again and were all cut down. *Lawhill* and *Pamir* sailed throughout the war years under the South African and New Zealand flags respectively, continuing to do so for a few more years afterwards. Both had been seized at the outbreak of the war by those countries in whose waters they happened to have been.

By 1946, freight rates on certain cargoes became profitable enough to make carriage by sail economically viable and even capable of returning a reasonable profit after the initial expenditure of refitting the ships. Gustaf Erikson, the famous Åland shipowner who before the war had the largest fleet of commercial square-riggers in the world, therefore decided in early 1946 to re-enter trade with his sailing ships. With a lot of swapping of gear and utilising that stored ashore from other ships, the *Viking* and *Passat* were able to be fitted out. Erikson's long-time London agents Clarksons were again used to facilitate the necessary liaison to operate international trading.

Viking was to load timber for South Africa, then coal for Santos in Brazil; it was hoped another cargo could then be acquired for Australia where a grain cargo was booked for delivery back to Europe. *Passat* was to load timber as well for South Africa, then try to obtain there a forward cargo to Australia before also sailing back with grain. This was an encouraging prospect, as in most cases, before the war, Erikson's ships sailed in ballast to Australia to pick up grain cargoes.

By this time the Baltic and the North Sea had been about swept clear of mines and sailing ships could hope to navigate out of these waters in relative safety. However, as well as having their foul bottoms scraped and repainted, the two vessels needed to have degaussing wires fitted as a precaution against any magnetic mines that might still be floating around.

So in the autumn of 1946 the two vessels left Mariehamn for dry-docking in Helsinki and this is where I met *Passat*.

*

I have tried to write this story for my fellow seamen as well as for all those who love the sea. As my main purpose was to record for posterity as much as I could of a way of life totally gone by, I could not avoid going at times into fairly elaborate details concerning the working of large sailing ships. I have tried to simplify slightly my description of the vessels' gear and of manoeuvres in the text of my narration for the benefit of uninitiated readers, and I have added three appendices which I hope will be found informative by those more curious of technical details.

Nevertheless, readers not familiar with nautical language may sometimes be puzzled and even overwhelmed by the abundance of specialised vocabulary and I call for their patience. Many details will gradually become clear as they read on. Most words likely to be unknown to non-sailors are explained in the Glossary. In the course of the narration, we have flagged some of these words with an asterisk at places where misunderstanding could create serious ambiguity. I trust that this Glossary, together with the footnotes and the many illustrations, will help everyone to feel at home with me on the good old ship *Passat*.

Chapter 1

JOINING THE *PASSAT*

I had always wanted to go to sea, from when I was a small lad, before the war. We lived in London just north of the Royal Docks. Whenever I could spare a few pence for the bus I would go down to the river at the docks entrance to watch the ships go in and out and pass by on the river.

We had at home an old sea chest that had belonged to an uncle who had become a hero to me, although I had never met him. He had done his time in British sailing ships, the *Elginshire* and *Kilmallie*. On the latter he had become third mate before he went ashore in the late 1920s, married and settled in Australia.

This chest was like a magic box to me. I can still remember the excitement I felt when opening it and contemplating the beautiful square-rigger that my uncle had painted inside the lid. It told of endless adventures and exotic pleasures, and I had no doubt I would be a seaman myself.

There was in fact no maritime tradition in our family, and it seems that Uncle Dick was a bit of a black sheep among my mother's relatives, for this and other reasons. We never talked about him.

When I expressed a wish to go to sea, I was vigorously told off by my father who wanted me to become a civil servant like him. However, we did not get on well and when I reached the age of sixteen he finally agreed to let me register at the Dock Street pool, pleased after all at getting rid of a rebellious youngster who was challenging his authoritarian grip on the household.

I therefore passed the Shipping Federation medical and soon afterwards signed up as a boy on a ship in the coastal trade. She was the *Serenity*, approximately 600 tons gross, one of Everard's of Greenhithe.

But I was especially mad about sail. I thought that in no time I would be able to swap to one of Everard's remaining sailing barges that I had seen. I soon realised that to be in between ships just at the time that a boy's job was going on one of these was like winning the pools.

After a couple of months at this second-best life I read about the Finnish shipowner Erikson fitting out two of his four-mast barques to go deep sea. I jumped at this chance and wrote away to Erikson for a berth on either of them.

There was some correspondence to and fro and after paying a hundred-pound bond to cover any expenses accrued by the owner if I deserted ship in a foreign country, I was accepted as an apprentice on the *Viking*.

I left Tilbury on the Swedish passenger ship *Grippsholm*, paying my own fare to Gothenburg. I was well kitted out for a two-year trip. My mother had knitted jumpers and socks for me. All my gear was in a sea bag and in Uncle Dick's sea chest.

I found Gothenburg a wonderful place. There were lots of oranges, bananas and chocolate on sale everywhere, delicacies that I had not had for years. I had time to have a quick look at the city as we had berthed first thing in the morning.

Then it was onto the train for the journey across Sweden to the capital Stockholm, where I stayed two days as I had missed the ferry to Åland. It was a beautiful city, especially the old town, Gamla Stan, and I enjoyed it after post-war London.

On the ferry then to Mariehamn where we did not arrive till late at night. With no one to meet me, and only speaking English, I was at a loss as to where to go. So leaving my gear at the terminal I walked up the town which was now deserted after the ferry passengers had gone to their homes.

I came up to a square, and as nothing was open, endeavoured to sleep on a park bench. It got very cold after a while as we were in October. By morning I was stiff and covered with a hoary frost. At last a shop opened and I warmed up with a cup of coffee.

At 9am I presented myself at Erikson's office where I was informed that the *Viking* was up in Vaasa loading and already had her complement anyway. I therefore was to join the *Passat*. This was all right by me, but I was worried when I learned that she had also left and that I would have to catch her up in the dry dock in Helsinki. I explained I had no more money for fares and was then told I would be accommodated for the night and be given vouchers for the ferry to Abo on the following day and then the train to Helsinki.

The rest of the morning I wandered around the town. In the afternoon I retraced my way back to the ferry terminal to check on my sea chest and to arrange my berth for the passage on the morrow.

In the daylight I could now view from the terminal a long stretch of the western harbour. As my gaze swept the foreshore my heart jumped. There, tied up alongside another wharf, was a big four-mast sailing ship. I was perplexed at this apparition since the two vessels I had knowledge of had departed.

With great excitement I soon made my way along the foreshore as if drawn by a magnet. Getting nearer I made out her name, *Pommern*. I walked the length of her along the wharf which was deserted. She was what was known as a 'bald-headed' four-mast barque, meaning that she did not cross royal yards above her topgallants.

There was a gangway leading up to her deck and as I could see no one around to bar me from boarding I was swiftly making a tour of her cluttered decks. She had a full-length well deck, that is, there was no midship castle but separate shelters, or deckhouses, for the crew accommodation, galley, donkey engine, etc. I went up on the forecastle head then aft to the poop. Still I found nobody about and I presumed that the workers had already knocked off since it was late afternoon.

I decided to try myself out at the task of going aloft. That would be a good practice run before joining the *Passat*. So I proceeded to climb each mast to the crosstrees, although I did not go out on the yards. This unexpected introduction to the 'true' sailing life was an exhilarating experience. I had the most gratifying feeling as I descended to the *Pommern*'s deck and walked back down the gangway.

I went to the boarding house to have a feed and an early night. The beds were made with crepe paper sheets, a new and strange experience for me. These were just burnt after use. Paper, a timber product, was in abundance in Finland whilst cotton sheets were unobtainable at that time. They were warm and comfortable and although they made a noise when you moved I slept deeply till morning.

Off again on another ferry to Abo, the old capital of Finland. Here I visited the old wooden three-masted barque *Sigyn*, moored alongside in the river. After a quick look around the town centre I jumped on the train for the last lap to Helsinki.

Again I arrived at night. I went to the central police station to ask for directions as no one I addressed in the streets spoke English. After an exciting period of watching detainees, mainly drunk, being dragged in fighting, charged and locked up, I was interviewed by an officer then put in a taxi and after collecting my gear from the station was off to the dry dock.

At last, there was the *Passat* with her masts looming up out of the mist in the glow of the dock arc lights and disappearing into the black above. I took my gear aboard and was helped by the night watchman to get my chest into the starboard forecastle. I was shown the after top bunk on the inboard side, which was to become my own few cubic feet of living space for the next two years.

Next day, 20th October 1946, I was signed on articles by the master, Captain Mattson, at the shipping office. Then it was immediately back to the ship and work.

I with the other first-trippers (my previous coaster experience not of course counting) were given menial tasks while in dry dock: cutting firewood for the forecastle stoves, pumping fresh water, cleaning heads (toilets).

The toilets and other overside discharges emptied into drums hung over the side whilst in dock, but they were now continuously freezing up. Many times I had to go over the side, sitting on a suspended plank (a 'bos'n's chair'), and poke away with a long rod at the discharge hole whilst hot water was poured down from above. The idea was to kick away as the melted contents gushed out, but our timing was not always correct and we often suffered the foul consequence.

We were however soon started on sailorising jobs up aloft, taking up the needed tools in our rigbags slung over one shoulder. These were like miniature sea bags. They were made of canvas with treble bottoms. The tools were wooden fids, marlin and splicing spikes, serving mallets, prikers, pliers and snippers. Also one carried spunyarn, marlin, sail twine and pieces of boltrope, seizing wire, sometimes even a block that could be needed for a repair or renewal job.

The rule was that we were shown once. Then if the job was not done correctly we were shown again with a warning of a whack around the ear or such. We caught on fast and the threat seldom had to be carried out. Such strict training is of course necessary, for tragic accidents can happen if a ratline or footrope or other item of rigging is not repaired or refitted correctly and gives way when taking a man's weight.

We also helped with the replacement of stays and other standing and running rigging that had deteriorated over the long lay-up.

On 2nd November, our bottom glowing with paint after scraping and our anti-mine degaussing wires fitted and girding the hull, the dock was filled and we were towed out. After clearing the port we were turned several times to check and correct our compasses and to test the anti-magnetic mine gear. Then we were off on our tow along the Gulf of Finland to Kotka.

There we loaded nearly a full cargo of sawn timber, 982 standards in all, 1,100 being our capacity. As pine timber is light, this was stowed over the 800 tons of granite ballast that had been left in the vessel for stability throughout the war lay-up.

We loaded at the main timber-mill wharf. This mill was huge, covering many acres. Our cargo was loaded in slings by crane. Then each plank was stowed by hand, all taking a long time. Women dockers made up the majority of the labour at this job.

The port was predominantly a timber one, but granite was also exported from there. Some wharves also handled general cargo. Ships from many nations came and went while we loaded.

I remember most the British and American ones, as I visited some to cadge food extras to supplement our meagre menu. From the UK's *Tilsington Court* I received marmalade, bread, tea and other delicacies.

However I had a memorable accident when departing her. Instead of stepping from the Jacob's ladder into our dinghy, I stepped onto the thin ice which under the weight of myself plus my haul stuffed down my coat and in the pockets gave way, and I sank into the icy water before I could grab the gunwale of the dinghy. Alas, I had tied the dinghy up to the ladder by the end of the painter, not short up, so it had drifted down the vessel's side. Fortunately, a line was thrown to me by the watchman who heard me shouting for help, and I made the deck blue with cold.

After thawing out and drying off my clothes in the ship's stokehold, I was about to put my clothes back on when I was confronted by an optimistic old deviate, the greaser on duty, who must have thought all his luck had come at once on beholding a young naked boy. I vigorously rejected his offer of a reward and made a hurried exit, clothes in hand, to inform the rest of the crew who roared with laughter on hearing of my encounter and the second escape from fate I had made aboard their vessel. This time I made a correct departure, intact so to say, and with replenished stores plus a much wiser outlook on the world and my fellow man.

From a US Lykes Line ship I secured a set of cotton sheets and pillowcases. So I was in luxury, as all that was issued to us on the *Passat* was a pillow, a kapok mattress and two grey blankets.

Winter was now on us and the snow and ice had set in. Rigging was a hard job with the lines frozen and hung with icicles. We had a meagre month while loading, as our boys' wages did not go far. Being an apprentice, mine were all but nil. However I was able to supplement them by re-selling my alcohol ration to the older men. Spirits were rationed at the time in Finland. Actually it was mainly wood alcohol. They got the headache and I got a little spending money.

On Saturday nights, unless I was watchman, I went up the town to see what 'lights' there were. I went to a couple of bars and dances. But without the language, short of funds and being under those conditions rather shy, I could only sit on a drink and fantasise about all the beautiful unattached blondes around. The US seamen had the time of their lives for they had plenty to spend. It must be realised that Finland after the war was in a bad way, with no luxuries and little food or amusement.

About this time another apprentice from England joined us, Adrian Small, or 'Pip'. I was glad to have the company of someone from home with whom I could converse. Some other crew members could speak a little English, but hardly enough to sustain any interesting conversation. Swedish was the spoken language on board. I gradually got by with some Swedish but in the end the other hands picked up English faster and in fact seemed reluctant to let us practise our faltering Swedish with them.

The same was not true for the officers. All orders were in Swedish, and they made it a point never to translate any for us, although the first and second mates were fairly proficient in English. As for the captain, who certainly had a good command of English, as needed for his official transactions in foreign ports, I never heard him pronounce an English word on board.

*

Passat was a typical example of the last deep-sea sailing vessels to ply the oceans commercially. She had been built in Germany in 1911 by Blom & Voss for the Hamburg shipowner F. Laeisz and had been part of the latter's famous Flying P Line (so named because all its vessels had names with initial P). Gustaf Erikson had bought her for a song in 1932. When I joined her she was therefore under the flag of Finland.

I was to sail on her before the mast as an apprentice the first year, then as OS ('Ordinary Seaman', in Swedish *Lättmatros*) towards the middle of the second year.

To be exact we were only 'before' the main mast as the port and starboard forecastles were situated in the fore part of the centre castle, on either side of the galley (kitchen). Such accommodation was a great improvement over that afforded under the forecastle head or in a deck house on the older-type vessels. In fact, the whole crew, including officers, was now quartered in the centre castle.

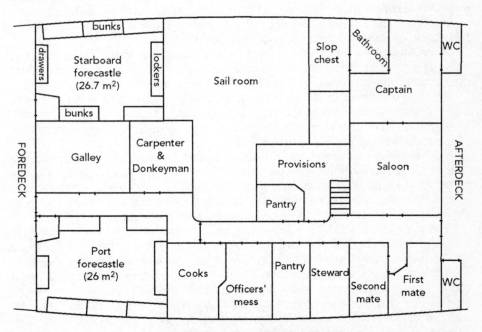

MIDSHIP ACCOMMODATION

Under the poop deck were eight state cabins for passengers, seldom used of course, and the saloon where the 'afterguard' (the officers) dined with the passengers. A flying bridge on the starboard side led from the forecastle head to the centre castle, and from there to the poop. This convenience was removed in port to give access to the hatches when the ship berthed with her starboard side to the wharf.

The expression 'afterguard' originates in the situation prevailing on the older flush-deckers. The poop used to house the officers, and the only rating allowed on this hallowed deck, except when some work had to be done there, was the helmsman who came and went via the leeside ladder. So this after section of all pre-three-island vessels was partially guarded in case of mutiny by restricting the number of men on the poop at any one time.

Our access to the forecastles was through top and bottom halved steel doors off the fore well deck* in good weather, or by skylight from the midship castle deck in bad weather, when the well decks were full of seas. Inside, the forecastles were identical. There was a small entrance housing the fresh water cask, which was filled each day for ten men's drinking purposes.

Water was severely rationed at sea and after it was allocated each morning the pump was locked. In tropical rain storms the scuppers and freeing ports, which drain water off the decks, were blocked and our tanks were replenished. After which bodies, bedding and clothes were washed.

There was also space in the entrance for hanging oilskins. Inside each forecastle were ten drawers forward, ten lockers aft, and double-tiered bunks, six outboard and four inboard with the galley serving hatch between them. Down the middle was the mess table with a bench seat on each side. At the head of the table was a bogey (stove) and wood box for warmth in cold weather. From the deck head hung an oil lamp. Daylight came from three portholes outboard and two more forward. After existing in such a hole battened down when allowed below in bad weather, it was wonderful to sleep out on deck in a hammock, or even on a hatch in good weather.

When fully manned, which was not always the case, *Passat* had a complement of thirty. They were master, three mates, carpenter, sailmaker, donkeyman, steward, cook, galley-boy, plus twenty forecastle hands.

All mates had been in sail before as a mate or second or third, most sailing in that category in sail before the war, and so had tickets (certificates) in sail. Masters, we had two over the period I was aboard, had both previously commanded sailing vessels of the company.

The sailmaker, carpenter and donkeyman were petty officers and they had a four-berth cabin and their own messroom. However, on this voyage, only the carpenter and the donkeyman occupied this cabin. The two spare bunks were intended for the sailmaker and his assistant, but our sailmaker remained with us in the starboard forecastle and he had no designated assistant.

The term 'donkeyman' is almost universally used for personnel in charge of running various engines on board ships. Around the 1890s, as the job of heaving up the anchor, sometimes both anchors, by man-operated capstan was becoming harder with bigger vessels and was found much too time-consuming, a small steam engine which powered a winch with barrel ends was installed on sailing vessels for that purpose. It was called a donkey boiler, or donkey engine, because of the practice current on mainly Yankee ships of using donkeys while in port to haul on lines and to lift cargo in or out. The seaman detailed to understand and run this device was of course given the engine's name. In addition to this function, the donkeyman also carried out minor blacksmithing and general metal work on board. On the *Passat* we had a later type engine, run on diesel oil. From the barrel end was run an endless wire up the foredeck to the barrel end of the windlass situated under the forecastle head and the capstan above. This hove up anchors in a fraction of the time it would have taken by hand. Our donkeyman, Marti Suomi, also maintained three cargo winches which also ran on diesel oil.

At sea, ships' crews are divided into teams, usually two, which alternate on duty, most commonly in spells of four hours. The term 'watches' refers both to these periods and to the teams themselves. These are commanded by the first and second mates respectively. Watches are set at the start of each voyage. The first mate has first pick, and the second mate the second choice of the forecastle hands.

On the *Passat* there were only four ABs ('Able-Bodied Seamen', in Swedish *Matros*). They were men who had sailed in square-rig before. We had six OSs (those had sailed in steam as ABs but also as such on fore-and-aft rigs). Then came us, the first-trippers, all lads of around 16 (on leaving Kotka a few more apprentices were still to join). So the two watches evened out: two ABs, three OSs and five boys in each.

Size and physique played a great part in the choices, so the mate had best choice in theory. Although some smaller fellows were more agile aloft, muscle was ever essential when heaving and hauling, furling sail, manning a capstan or steering with a kicking wheel.

Although they were key hands on the vessel, the donkeyman, the carpenter and the sailmaker were normally 'idlers' or day workers, except in heavy weather when at times they had to lay aloft. The fact that our sailmaker was part of a watch during my time on the *Passat* was exceptional.

Occasionally it was all hands on deck, including the steward, cook and galley-boy, but these did not go aloft, helping on deck instead and so releasing others to go aloft. So at sea all worked twelve hours per day on watches.

Maintenance work was performed between 6am and 5pm Monday to Friday and between 6am and 1pm on Saturdays.

Watches always assembled and were counted at the watch change, the wheel and lookout being relieved before the 'off watch' went below. Often the off watch in fact spent part or the whole of their 'off' time up aloft taking in sail when there was a blow and sail had to be reduced quickly.

I soon found that 'working' the vessel carried on twenty-four hours per day. This meant making and taking off sail, bracing and trimming yards, bending new sails, tacking and wearing* ship, steering and lookout. The watch below could be called on deck at any time, to take in sail or to assist in any way whenever the watch on deck could not cope safely with the urgent work demanded by heavy weather. However, when possible, reducing sail was carried out at the change of watch, when all hands were on deck.

There was no overtime in sail. One cursed, but never argued. The overriding rule was 'give your best or founder'. This existence of sleeping when you could and seldom out of wet gear, often in your oilskins, sometimes lasted for a month. There was no other way in winter on the routes taken by sailing ships to obtain the necessary winds to make the fastest possible time on each voyage. We all knew that we had to take the good with the bad, or pay off if allowed to (and if not then 'skin out').

While in Kotka we sorted out our suits of sails and bent the best set, the newest and strongest, one by one to their respective yards, and carried on with the repair and maintenance of the standing and running rigging. This was a crucial operation as all the rigging had deteriorated over the long lay-up during the war.

The state of disrepair of the running gear was very obvious, as lines were carrying away with little strain put on them. Ratlines gave way as we climbed aloft, sometimes three or four at a time, giving us a sudden unexpected drop. We soon learned to hold onto the shrouds when going aloft. Eventually, all had to be gradually renewed, the worst ones before we sailed.

The deterioration of the flexible wire was harder to ascertain, parts often being hidden with serving*. Standing rigging was also guesswork, but where deterioration or serious wear was obvious, the stays were renewed so as to enable the vessel to start the long voyage in comparative safety and carry enough sail to push her along. Being careful not to put too much strain at first on her tophamper we would gradually complete the renovation work while under way.

After brief instruction and demonstration, all new hands were expected to go anywhere aloft, in fact the youngest and lightest were expected to handle the highest, but of course the smallest sails, and to go furthest out on all yardarms when handling the larger sails, the older hands sticking to the bunt.

Quickly also was memorised the sequence of lines belayed on the pin and fife rails, so that on the blackest of nights we hauled on the correct line and never threw off a wrong line. There were over 250 lines and belaying pins, 29 miles of running rigging to contend with that all had an essential purpose.

Passat had the three major labour-saving devices that were installed on later sailing vessels. They were four deck capstans, geared halyard winches for the upper topsail and upper topgallant yards, and Jarvis brace winches which turned the three heavy yards on each square sail mast before trimming. They were all operated by hand, of course. These devices allowed for smaller crews, so they meant savings for the owner, not for us!

The steering wheel was midships on the centre castle, with another used in emergency directly over the rudder post on the poop. Both were double wheels with a grating each side so up to four helmsmen could, at either position, hold the vessel on course. With a big sea running, we would pass over the shoulder a 'kick strap' which was anchored to the grating; otherwise we would be sent flying by the rudder's kick and let the wheel spin out of control, possibly putting the vessel aback and causing serious damage even to the extent of dismasting. We learnt very smartly the many dangers of such vessels and the precautions to take so as not to be maimed or lost overboard.

*

The loading was at last completed. The lower hold was packed tight with timber to deck head and the 'tweendeck almost full too. At least with such a buoyant cargo we would never sink! Hatches were battened down, the main, mizzen and jigger forestays reset up after being dropped for the cranes while loading, the yards trimmed and the decks squared up.

On a cold blustery dull day in early December, a tug towed us off our berth and into the channel cleared of ice by the ice-breakers employed around the Baltic in winter to keep ports open and trade continuing the year around. Alas, a first setback occurred here.

There was very little room to manoeuvre in the channel and we did not have any means of propulsion to counter the effect of the current and the wind on the hull. One tug was clearly insufficient to pull our considerable deadweight, and we went aground.

The next day at high tide a second tug came to our assistance and we were hauled off. Later soundings found we had not taken water and further inspections of the plates resulted in us being declared fit to proceed.

We departed from Kotka again and proceeded under the tow of two tugs along the coast towards Hango. the end of the ice-cleared channel and the open sea. From there we were to set sail and, at last under our own means, make for Karlshamn in the Blekinge area of south Sweden.

All went well till nearly up to Hango. We were making about six knots down the channel. I was assisting an AB and learning to steer at the wheel. The pilot gave an order to the tugs that he was altering course to port. This order was relayed by megaphone. He ordered the necessary wheel to be put on to bring us round to the new course. Both the port tug and *Passat* went to port.

But the starboard tug must have mistaken the order and it went to starboard. She was the *Lovisa* of Rauma, a big ocean-going tug with a crew of twelve. The inevitable happened: with our weight and that of the other tug both pulling nearly at right angle to the *Lovisa*, she was put on her beam ends where she hung for a moment, then to our horror she was dragged right over and under the water.

The steel wire tow line was for a few moments jumping on our forward bitts, throwing off a shower of sparks. Our chippy, realising what was occurring, raced to his locker, grabbed his axe, and tried to sever the line. But it was all too late for we were dragging the *Lovisa* along the bottom of the channel.

The other tug stopped pulling and was let go from us to steam round to the rescue. Chippy, donkeyman, a mate and a couple of hands dropped both anchors so as to pull us up, which took some time. The rest including me were ordered to launch a lifeboat.

We tried to swing one out but the davits would not turn. The same with the second boat: the davits had rusted solid in their sockets. We tried with all our might, even breaking a capstan bar in the process, but to no avail, we could not take part in the rescue.

The other tug picked up three survivors, two of which I had watched scrambling up the *Lovisa*'s side as she turned over. The other nine crew were drowned in her.

This second catastrophe was not a good omen for the start of the long voyage ahead of us. We hove up our anchors using the donkey engine, and were towed back to Helsinki where we anchored off for a few days while our master and the pilot went ashore to attend a marine inquiry into the accident. I cannot remember the exact outcome of this except that there was no blame attributed to our captain.

Shore workers came out and did hot work on all eight davits, freeing them up. We lifted them and greased them well. We all had the same thought on our mind: what if this accident had not taken place? The state of the davits would not have been found and rectified, and if later we had had to use the lifeboats for a rescue at sea or to abandon ship, we would have had no chance.

Eventually we were cleared and sailed for Karlshamn on Friday the 13th. Our spirits were very low and to have to sail on such an ominous date added to our gloom.

The run across the Baltic was rather uneventful considering our previous record, except that our third mate died. No one knew for certain the cause of death. It may have been related to his drinking the wood alcohol heavily, which was an unfortunate occupation of many in Finland at that time.

We set topsails and foresail before dropping the tug after passing Hango, a Russian naval base. The Finnish nation, which was a member of the Axis, had been through an unstable situation since it got out of the war in 1944. The Russians, although not occupying Finland, took eastern Karelia and were the dominant neighbour. A few of their warships came to see us set sail, and I suppose wondered at such a sight in 1946.

The winds were favourable and with some tacking under full sail we made Karlshamn in two days. We saw the *Viking* ahead of us beating south off Gottland. She was coming down from Vaasa. She docked six hours ahead of us. So both were again in the same port for a few days.

In Karlshamn we loaded stores that had been too expensive or unobtainable in Finland at that time. We took on paint, more wire rope, coils of fibre cordage, etc. The steward stocked up with ship biscuits, tins of fish balls, dried stockfish, sausage, salted meat and vegetables that would keep for a while, for we had no refrigeration. We also took on six sheep, four pigs and some chickens, all live, for fresh food on the coming voyage. Pens for these were built under the forecastle head by four local carpenters under the supervision of our chippy.

Purchased also was kerosene for our lamps and sidelights, fuel for the donkey engine and the winches, and coal for the galley. A layer of heavy 12-by-4-inch planks cut to the length of the hatches was laid over the three tarps on each hatch, which had all been battened and wedged. Over these planks were drawn wire and chain lashings through the eye rings on the hatch coamings, and all were then drawn bar-tight with bottle screws and stoppered off. So we were well battened down against the heaviest seas.

Four more apprentices joined, plus another third mate, giving us a full crew. Two of the new lads were from England. Martin Lee was from Shoreham and

Terry Dwyer was, like me, from London. Both had been to a navigation school. The other two were Swedes from Stockholm and were a bit older than us. They were Karl Berglund and Hakon Hammer, both naval cadets put on reserve for the duration of our voyage to South Africa.

Martin joined me in the starboard watch and Terry went into the port with Pip. The two Swedes wanted to stay together and a swap enabled them to go both into the port watch.

So our master and mate were from Åland, and the second and third mates from Abo. The forecastle hands apart from the apprentices were (except for one deck-boy from Åland) from other ports and places in Finland. Two ABs were Swedish Finns and two were Finns. One of the latter became the sailmaker. The carpenter was a Swedish Finn and the donkeyman a Finn. Six of the deck-boys were Finns, the others Swedish Finns. And we had one Finnish OS. We were also carrying twelve passengers, the majority of whom were from Finland.

The Åland Islands were part of Sweden till after the First World War. Also Swedes had been settled around the coast of Finland for several hundred years, and these spoke mainly Swedish although a few also spoke Finnish. So the majority of the crew were bilingual, making it all the more difficult for us four boys from Britain to ever learn. As the orders, as I said, were always in Swedish we soon became conversant with them. If they had been in Finnish we would have been hopeless on board for a long time as this seems to be about the most difficult language to learn.

At this time Captain Mattson left us. None of us ever found out the actual reason for his departure. It certainly had nothing to do with his ability for he was respected for his seamanship and considered a fair and dedicated sailing-ship master. Unsettled perhaps by the catastrophes we had already experienced, he may have felt rather daunted by the prospect of taking such a run-down vessel on such a voyage, the duration of which was unknown, with a crew in large part constituted of first-trippers or men with no sail training, and with the added responsibility of passengers.

To illustrate the lack of experience of the crew, it is worth mentioning that we had received no training at lifeboat drill or at abandon-ship routine, even though such exercises were made mandatory by all countries' maritime laws.

Captain Mattson was relieved by Captain Hagarstrand, also a very capable officer. Both had commanded Erikson's sailing vessels over many years before the war. Mauritz Mattson had commanded *Penang* (in 1925–1931), then *Olivebank* and *Pamir*. Iver Hagerstrand went back even further and was master of the *Loch Linne* in 1923–1924, after which he commanded the *Woodburn*, *Hougamont*, *Winterhude* and *Viking*.

We had some more metalwork repairs carried out while alongside, which took us up to New Year, giving us Christmas or *Jultidning* in Scandinavia, and in port. This was quite an event. We cleared the decks of snow and dressed the vessel as best we could with fir-tree branches at all four mastheads and the jib-boom. A few badly furled sails were re-done and all the yards trimmed exactly right. Many visitors came aboard to wish us well, some even bringing little presents. They were very kind to the young crew members and we did our best to show off the *Passat*.

Chapter 2

INTO THE ATLANTIC

At last on 2nd January 1946 we departed Sweden with happy memories. The *Viking* had sailed about 28th December.

We towed off our berth at Karlshamn, made sail and cast off the tow. We were on our way on a real voyage. Two men were needed at the wheel in the enclosed waters we were entering. This was an opportunity to give the apprentices some practice at steering. We came into the Sound with plenty of tacking but in the end dropped anchor off Copenhagen because of headwinds and lack of room to manoeuvre. We hoped there were no sea mines floating around from here till we were out and clear of the North Sea.

A wind change at last allowed us to weigh anchor and sail into the Kattegat and then the Skagerrak. Soon we took our last landfall off Skagen in north Denmark, and then we were into the North Sea and soon out of sight of land.

We were now able to take in both anchors, which were still hanging on the catheads* over each side of the forecastle after being fished when departing the Kattegat. They were lifted onto the forecastle head by the crane and screwed down. The chains were unshackled from the anchors, lowered back over the side, then drawn in through the hawse pipes by the capstan and paid down the spurling pipes, which led to the chain lockers. One man, down the locker, flaked the chain neatly as it came down. A wire was bent onto the joining shackle at the end of the chains and tied off near the top of the spurling pipes, which were finally plugged with wooden caps, cemented over and clamped.

It had been decided not to risk taking the short course through the English Channel because of the heavy shipping movements and the possible danger of stray mines. Instead we would go north about into the Atlantic, then sail well to the westward before turning south, clear of Eire, and look for the NE trade winds at about 20° north.

Westerly gales prevented us from going around the north of Scotland and drove us far to the north of the Shetlands and even to the north of the Faeroes, where we beat against continuous headwinds. It was hard going and bitterly cold, as January is the worst month of winter up in those latitudes. We clawed our way gradually west towards Iceland in order to get clear of land or islands, hoping then to be able to go at last on a running starboard tack heading south for the trades. Alas this hope was not fulfilled for a very long time and in fact might well never have been realised at all. Further and further fell the glass, and we knew we were in for a blast.

We were trying to reduce down to lower topsails and all hands had been up aloft for hours furling sail when a full-blown Atlantic hurricane savagely struck just south of Iceland. Before we could get any more sails in, we had lost six of them blown clean out their bolt ropes.

We were pinned to the yard for long agonising moments and all we could do was hang onto the jackstay holding the canvas, which was like sheet iron, between our belly and the yard till we could at last grasp the sail's foot and roll it up onto the yard. Countless times we would almost win, only to lose from our grasp the already won canvas, which filled again with a clap of thunder.

To make matters worse, and our almost impossible task more difficult, the vessel was heeling over dangerously despite the reduced sail area on her. It was only after hours of a terrible contest aloft by every available man that we got her shortened down to fore and main lower topsails, foremast staysail and brailed-in spanker. In the end we were so numb with fatigue that I did not know what day it was or whether it was day or night.

We were braced well around and hove to* on the port tack and all prayed that nothing carried away aloft and started the horrific process of dismasting. On deck, no one could stand against the wind which had reached tremendous force and was building up the already heavy sea into mountainous proportions.

The wave crests were blown straight ahead to become spume, so that sea and sky appeared one and we could hardly see or talk. We disappeared into the troughs of the huge waves enjoying a few seconds' relief from the force threatening to overwhelm us, then up we rose to the oncoming next wave crest, to take the full blast of the hurricane again.

Four men were needed at the wheel to hold the ship and stop her from coming up into the wind. This would have put aback what sails we had still set and put so much strain on the forestays as to dismast her. Our old rigging was certainly going to be tested to the full.

After a superhuman effort by the four helmsmen to control her steering it was found she was becoming more sluggish in answering the helm and that she was broaching* onto the oncoming seas.

We were soon being pushed over onto our beam ends by the combination of the pressure of wind on the scant sail area we had, and the force of the huge waves now striking us broadside. The angle became horrific, the lower yardarms now dipping into the seas. It was hopeless to try to walk, for the starboard gunwales were under the seas which were lapping over the leeside of the hatches.

In all this, every so often, along with the roar of the hurricane, came the pitiful screams of the injured and drowning animals from their pens under the forecastle head. The scene was unreal. We had been thrown into Dante's *Inferno*.

At daylight, which was very little better than night, the carpenter was able to get forward during a short lull. It could be observed now that the ship was down by the head, and from the soundings taken by the chippy it appeared that the forepeak was full of sea. The two spurling pipes and two vent bases, that we had plugged and covered, had been opened up by the seas coming over the forecastle head. They led straight down to the forepeak and had allowed it to fill. This was then the cause of the helm failing to steer us and the reason for broaching to.

No one had been off deck for the last two nights and a day so we took shelter behind the weatherside bulwark of the centre castle. The wheel was now useless and was lashed hard over. I vividly remember also lashing myself to the pin rail, in the refuge I mentioned, so as to rest without having to hang on by hand. Any one who let go would have skidded down the deck and probably over the leeside into the sea.

Raising my head above the gunwale I watched the massive walls of the waves coming towards us. Slowly, we would rise and rise whilst being pushed over even further, until the crest of the wave, lapping at the windward gunwales, at last passed under us. Then we would right a little, with a sickening lurch, to then again descend to the bottom of the trough and the oncoming next wave. And so endlessly.

How long could we last in such a predicament? Would we manage to survive this new calamity or be turned right over? What a way to end such a short life! No one would really know what became of us as there was no radio to send a 'May-Day' distress call. The vessel would not sink if turned over but we had no hope of survival in those seas, as no lifeboat could be launched, and none would be able to stay afloat anyway. In fact the two starboard lifeboats had already disappeared.

All this time we had only partaken of coffee and cold food from the officers' mess and a few tots of brandy to keep our spirits up, as the galley was out of action. The list made it impossible to hold anything on the stove, and furthermore the cook had also been on deck most of the time.

Two things were necessary to extricate us from this perilous position. We had to reduce our sail area even more, then empty the forepeak and thus bring the ship's head up allowing her to steer again and thereby fall off from the wind direction and right herself. The first objective was realised without our intervention when the windward sheet of the fore-topsail broke just under the foreyard.

This chain end was now being whipped by the force of the released sail, in a fearful arc, smashing into all that was in its reach, and sending showers of sparks flying as it hit steel. This new menace had to be contained at any cost; otherwise it could very soon bring down the foremast. As a matter of fact, it was seen that a forestay had already parted, owing to the mast being savagely jerked.

The lethal chain had to be caught and secured. One of the Finnish lads, with great bravery, went out on the weather yardarm, and with his knife cut the head of the sail away from the jackstay as far as the bunt while continually ducking the whipping chain. This deed allowed us to catch and smother the chain. A lashing was then put around the sail in the bunt, so technically we had a goose-winged lower topsail, which eased the angle of the list slightly. However the forepeak would have to wait awhile.

At this stage the starboard watch hands received some even more demoralising news: one of the lads had lifted the skylight hatch to go down and fetch something, only to find our forecastle nearly full of sea washing violently from side to side as the vessel lurched. Apparently two of the porthole glasses had cracked and, even though the deadlights were down, this had allowed the sea to enter continuously over our long absence. So we would have no bunks to go to, no dry gear to change into.

As there was now little more that anyone could do in our condition, the port watch was sent below for sleep, if they could get such, for even with the high bunk boards, those in the weather side bunks would have had to wedge themselves in to prevent falling out with the list. Then it was our turn and we were admitted as temporary refugees into the sail locker. This was five-star paradise and we at last slept for four hours.

By the next day the hurricane had passed but although the wind had eased the seas were still as huge. With the wind pressure reduced *Passat* righted herself, allowing us to take stock of the damage. She looked all but a floating wreck, down by the head and still listing, but no one had been lost or injured to any extent.

The following day saw us wallowing in a massive sea but a light wind. Now was the time for action and from then on day after day we worked, watch and watch, trying to pump out the forepeak. Six of the fittest of our twelve passengers were press-ganged during daylight hours to man the forward pump, so relieving a team of us in turns to square up the mess aloft and on deck. To leeward was a mass of tangled lines streaming over the bulwarks and out through the freeing ports. Those that had been coiled on the weather pin rails were also across the deck and were entangled with others. All of course were swollen, all had to be cleared and recoiled.

Aloft were blocks swinging on pendants with no lines reeved through. The remnants of the sails that had blown out had to be sent down and new sails sent up, bent and furled or set.

The pump was continually blocking. When the forepeak was filling all the stores, paint, Stockholm tar, kerosene, coils of fibre rope, etc., had mixed with the sea water forming a gooey, lumpy mess that blocked the inlet pipe. The latter was in a strum box and inaccessible. The problem was solved by going in under the main deck in the forepeak, separating the top of the suction pipe from the pump and fitting a rubber hose in its place with a weight affixed on its end so as to suck the water from near the top. Each time the hose blocked we were able to haul it out and clear it.

With a lot of clearing and repriming, we continued this backbreaking task round the clock. There were approximately 500 tons of water to be emptied. The pump was manned by teams of six, four men at the handles helped by two others at lines that we ran from these handles. After a few days at this exercise, and with the weather moderating and the sea going down, the list diminished markedly and our trim also started to rectify.

Soon we were able to have control with the helm and with some bracing of the yards, on which several original and fresh sails were now bent and set, we payed off running before the wind and a big westerly swell. After another few days of slow progress in distance but improvement in the vessel's general condition, having lowered the ullage mark considerably in the forepeak, we at last went on the opposite tack. We then steered as near a southerly course as we could, hoping for an early pick up of the NE trades.

Another week of improvement all around saw us under topgallants, in the latitude of Spain, and looking for the trade winds. During this time, apart from our normal duties and the forepeak emptying, we in the starboard watch had been able at last, now that we were on a more even keel with only a sea now and then coming on deck, to open the steel doors to our 'home' and drain the sea out.

There was not much left of any use inside. Some of our drawer contents were still intact, but the mattresses had been mashed up and their fibres, along with splinters from the disintegrated bunk boards, had infiltrated the drawers and lockers, and could even be found between the pages of every book. The bunk posts were bent. Very little was saved from the sodden mass that we pulled out on deck.

Apart from what I wore at the time I went on deck before the hurricane, I had nothing retrievable in clothing, as my sea chest had been smashed to bits. After scrubbing out the forecastle we left it to dry out for some days. Meanwhile our busy carpenter, who was mending and making new blocks as well as repairing many other smashed wooden objects, found time, with the help of a couple of Finns in our watch who were handy with his tools, to measure up new bunk boards and bases along with a new mess table and benches. We straightened out the metal posts with the help of the donkeyman.

When all was dry, aired and refitted, we moved back in, but with only makeshift mattresses made with anything we could cadge.

By the end of January we had been a month out from port and were into the trade winds at last. We now started getting into a proper shipboard routine. The sea was all but out of the forepeak and we came to the nasty job of separating what was retrievable from the stinking toxic magma at the bottom.

Braving the fumes, we sorted out what were once coils of various sized wire, untangled these down the deck, cleaned them off and recoiled them. The coils of fibre rope were of course useless and they were dumped with the rest of the mess. The bulkheads* and ceiling* were cleaned off and made ready for repainting when we acquired replacement stores. What a filthy job it was! At times we nearly passed out with the fumes as there were no fans or masks in those times.

We had much difficulty cleaning this sticky grime off ourselves. There was little kerosene left for this use, and no soft water over our normal daily ration. We had to make do with salt water and saltwater soap.

By this time our vegetables had gone rotten and were dumped. The lack of fresh food naturally started an outbreak of boils. These, in a few cases, developed into severe infections when they were chafed while working in the filth I have described. I felt very lucky never to suffer these for I saw the discomfort of those who did.

To help with keeping healthy and clean, most of us submitted to the long-voyage tradition, for boys at least, on German and Scandinavian sailing ships, of having our heads shaved. Eino Lackman, an older AB, was the barber. All but one in our watch were shorn, so Martin and I complied. Only half of the port watch submitted to losing their locks.

The weather now was becoming a sailor's dream, pretty constant wind from the one direction, giving us far less brace work and easier night watches. Soon we changed from the old four-hours-on / four-hours-off system to the 'Swedish' watch system of two four-hour watches, two five-hour ones and a six-hour one, within each twenty-four hours. This gave each watch a good six-hour rest every second day. The times were midnight–0400, then 0400–0800, then 0800–1300, then 1300–1900 and 1900–midnight.

Alas our night sojourns were soon cut down as another fair-weather sailing tradition was soon applied so as to gain the maximum productivity out of us would-be loafers. From each watch four men were taken off watch-keeping duties and put onto day work. Our fair-weather routine, unless interrupted by tropical storms, hurricanes or cyclones in the Pacific, lasted from entering the latitudes of the NE trades through the 'doldrums', a region spanning a few degrees both sides of the equator (with some variation in different oceans) where there was very little wind, then through the SE trades till the 'horse latitudes' where the winds became variable and fully manned watches were needed again.

Of the eight hands going on day work, one with a bent and ability for woodwork would be chippy's assistant, repairing damaged parts of the vessel's timberwork, including the countless blocks, and decking (caulking). Another, who had a basic understanding of a blacksmith's work and would have volunteered for the job, assisted our donkeyman at his forge under the forecastle. He repaired all the smaller metal rigging parts and even made new ones. The other six would assist the sailmaker, whose task was always formidable and was at that particular time nigh impossible.

None of the 'foreigners' were chosen for day work on this voyage. One of the reasons why I was never chosen was that I am left-handed. When sewing canvas all my stitches went the wrong way, which was unthinkable. I was only allowed to work at repairing old sails.

In each watch four lads were made 'topmen'. Each had his own mast to look after on his respective side, port or starboard. I had the mizzen and was responsible for overhauling and renewing lighter running and standing rigging (footropes, shrouds, buntlines, rovings, etc.) with help when necessary. Each topman, when not assisting with the sailing of the vessel, the wheel or on other big jobs, would spend his working time up his mast at these tasks, for the whole daylight watch, and sometimes over the watch change when a job had to be completed on an item that had to be ready for use at any time.

Now that we were well into the trades, the main job each day for a while was changing heavy-weather sails, those less used and therefore stronger, for fair-weather ones, old sails that would still stand up to the moderate force of the trade winds without tearing, but ones that also could be sacrificed to the wear they would suffer in the doldrums. In regions of highly variable winds sails are subjected to much chafing when they continually fill then come aback with the sound of thunder in the constant swell that rolls the vessel from side to side.

We hauled all the old sails out of the locker, a heavy job with the big ones, and they were all inspected and retagged. One I remember, a topsail, was from our sister ship the *Peking*. It had the date 1922 marked on the clew. Gustaf Erikson had tendered to buy that ship too at one time but missed out. However he had purchased, for a bargain, the whole best set of sails from her, knowing they would fit the *Passat*.

One by one the good sails were sent down on a gantline* and old ones sent back up in their place. It was at this job that I soon decided to wear a hat when up aloft in the sun, as with no hair left to protect my scalp I became dizzy after a while, a dangerous situation when high above deck.

There were now plenty of porpoises around, playing ahead of our stem. Bonitoes were in abundance also, chasing flying fish, quite a few of which landed on deck. Our chippy, Franz Forsman, showed us how to catch bonito by trailing a coloured rag on a hook from the end of the jib-boom. A few were caught and proved very palatable. They were a welcome addition to our menu. We needed fresh food now that we were only fed dried or salted fare.

Three of the sheep had survived drowning but they had to be put down as soon as possible owing to their broken legs and other injuries. For a few days, as long as the meat stayed fresh in the warming climate, we got offcuts and blood pudding, the passengers and afterguard dining on the best cuts, of course.

Food is a most important matter on board a ship. A sailor's life can be tolerable or miserable depending on the quality and quantity of the rations. On this voyage the quality was wanting while the quantity was just sufficient to sustain the energy required of us each day. The cook's lot was a hard one. With limited resources, he had two fares to cater for, the saloon then the forecastles.

There was no refrigeration and enough provisions had to be carried to last for periods of up to six months and more. This made the steward's provedoring a vital task, but a difficult one because he had to work on a very low budget allocated by a vigilant shipowner. So sugar and butter (tinned) were rationed for us. We had hard rye bread in packets on demand but fresh bread baked only on Sunday. Sausage, tinned fish balls, stockfish and raw salted herring were our staple meals, with the occasional blood pudding or fatty stew when an animal was slaughtered.

Our main stores were from Finland where, as I said, the fare ashore was very plain and meagre. Some jam, marmalade, pickles and other delicacies were taken on in Sweden but the cost restricted such luxuries to the saloon. On later voyages the food quality improved when tinned vegetables were available at a lower price. However there was always a lack of fresh food and on the first voyage many of the lads were covered with boils.

At last we experienced our first Sunday at sea without work except for our trick at the wheel and lookout and the usual trimming of yards and overhauling of buntlines*[1]. All got going washing ourselves, then our clothes, with water caught from a rain squall. We were even able to sunbathe and our clothes dried in minutes.

Soon we ran out of the NE trades and entered the monotonous and objectionable doldrums. There were days of being becalmed, just rolling in the swell and making no headway, except with the current which could take us in a direction opposite to our desired course. On occasions we swam over the side, with shark watchers posted of course. It was dive in and swim back straight to the Jacob's ladder and out. However it cooled one off and broke the monotony.

Day after day the rain would pour down in torrents, giving us surplus fresh water but not even steerage way. On some days there would be a shark-catching session. The donkeyman made a few hooks on which wire traces were spliced.

---

[1] See Appendix 3.

They were baited with some rotten meat and trailed over the side on a line. Many sharks of a good size were hooked and hauled aboard. They had a capstan bar inserted in their jaws and their tails roped to hold them still while they were dispatched and cut up. The largest tail was nailed to the end of the jib-boom to conjure up a favourable wind. Some of the skins went to making knife sheaths and other articles.

The donkeyman showed us how to take out the 'backbone' cartilage, insert a metal rod right through it and when it dried out, lacquer it. After that a thread was cut on the top and bottom of the rod, to screw onto the top a brass handle and to the bottom end, a brass tip. The finished result was a fine walking stick.

During this period we finished the clean-up of the forepeak. Other work was mending sails under cover. Then as we drifted south we incurred deceptive cat's-paws of wind and we had to brace continually to take advantage of every one.

Progressing slowly south, we eventually reached the equator. We were not informed when exactly we crossed 'the Line' but for reasons of work productivity it happened coincidentally on a Saturday afternoon.

As we cleaned up after work, who should pay us a visit from forward over the jib-boom, but King Neptune and all his court! A canvas wading pool had previously been erected alongside No. 2 hatch on the foredeck for us to jump into and cool off when on watch below. To this vicinity the royal troop headed and their attendants set up their thrones on the hatch.

The royal court consisted of Neptune himself, his queen, his doctor, his barber, the high priest and the policemen. The latter's role was to handle any stubborn or unruly first-trippers who tried to evade the ordination of joining the fraternity of deep-water sailors and becoming Neptune's subjects.

All of us, first-trippers and coastal sailors, were assembled before his majesty, then knelt on the hatch as our names were called. Each was castigated by the high priest for his past unseamanlike habits. The King then passed his verdict of the sentence that would induce us to behave in the future, once over the line, in a correct nautical fashion. Each 'candidate' in turn was held by the policemen whilst first the barber lathered up his face with a black foam and then shaved this off with a two foot wooden cut-throat razor, and then the doctor poured a horrible concoction down his throat. Any mouth that did not at first willingly open soon did after seeing one uncooperative lad have his head ducked into a bucket of vile liquid by a policeman. Next our heads, chests and other intimate parts were brushed with Stockholm tar and linseed oil, to preserve us it was said. Finally we were flipped over backwards into the canvas pool from whence we slunk away to suffer our indignity while trying to somehow clean our bodies and wash our mouths out.

Only one big strong lad, Elmer from Åland, refused to come out and attend. He had to be dragged out from the forecastle by the policemen and the second mate. The latter used excessive force and punched him. So as soon as this lad was able to break free in the ceremony, he retaliated, and it became a vicious fight between him and the second mate, who fancied himself as a knuckle man. The lad eventually got a bear hug on the second, after being pretty cut about. The policemen intervened at this stalemate and laid them both out with their belaying pin 'truncheons'. This was the end of the ceremony anyway and the royal troop retired aft taking the second mate with them.

So, all in all, it was an eventful day only marred at the finale. After we had cleaned up as best we could, we were later called aft, one by one, and given a tot of brandy and a certificate signed by Neptune that we had graduated to being deep-watermen and his new subjects.

*

Drifting brought us ever nearer the Brazilian coast and looking for the SE trades. At last, after a few pretenders, we picked up a good southeaster and were once again laying over under a full press of canvas, and by 17th February were averaging seven knots in a position approximately 300 miles off the coast of South America.

Since the battering we took in the North Atlantic we had been making approximately eighteen inches of water in the main bilges each day and so for a while we also manned the main pumps on the foredeck abaft the foremast. It took us a good three hours' spell at the pumps to take the water out. However once the donkey engine was overhauled after we got on an even keel again, it was primed, started, connected to the pumps and emptied us dry in one hour each day. We hoped that the fuel not lost down the forepeak would hold out till port.

We were told that a plate had been sprung, when grounding off Kotka, but that it had not loosened up till we were laid over on our side, during the hurricane, when the stresses on the hull, both inside and out, were all diametrically altered.

The two ABs had now finished repairing our main lower topsail, almost from scratch, so this was the last sail we changed, the old having stood up well. The sailmaker had also repaired the spanker, but we left on the one bent as it was in good shape and equivalent now to the repaired one.

Lackman, one of the ABs, who had an unpredictable fuse, gave one of the Swedish apprentices a cuffing round both ears, for talking back to him. I myself had fallen foul of the Finns early on by bragging about the UK having the best merchant marine and the best seamen. Of course such foolish boasting to men whose nation had kept sail on the high seas till then, was like a red rag to bulls. I learned my lesson the hard way, often being left on the forecastle head in heavy weather, when on lookout, for several hours instead of one. It was not until Cape Town that my sin was forgotten.

As we had plenty of red lead in the deck store, our job for the next few days was chipping, scraping and leading on the after-deck bulwarks and hatch coamings. All this would be painted with grey, black and white topcoats when paint could be purchased in port.

We sighted land one day. It was South Trinidad and we passed a good distance off to leeward. It was on the horizon all day, but by next morning was out of sight even from a royal yard. We were still holding onto the SE trades which was unusual for the 'horse' latitudes. By 28th February the winds petered out, leaving us drifting with the current in the right direction at 2–3 knots.

The food was very bad by this time as we were 60 days out. That night we sighted a ship's lights and this gave us something to discuss other than the food and our wretched predicament. We saw some albatrosses, a sign that a fair wind was not far away. Sure enough, around latitude 28° south we graciously received the westerlies. At Lat. 32° S, Long. 24° W, we squared away fully SE under all sail for the Cape.

We went on with our painting preparations, now starting work on the foredeck, but soon the wind strengthened and the watches, now back to ten men

each, stood by when working, ready for the two whistles that would call us to
shorten sail.

On 9th March, the weather deteriorating, we were on standby at all times.
The port watch took in the main and mizzen royals. We took in the fore royal.
In the afternoon watch we took in the mizzen upper topgallant, and the port
watch took in the fore and main ones when they came on deck at the change of
watch.

Early on the following morning, at watch change, both watches took in the
crossjack and mainsail. The mate gave us the job of chipping under the catwalk.
I was holding a scraper in my left hand when at an extra pitch I fell off the stage
that we had rigged and forgetting to throw the scraper clear, cut my wrist badly
on landing on the deck. Our captain cleaned the wound up with peroxide and
bandaged it up, telling me to be careful when scraping with my other hand. So
back to work.

Just on watch change the main lower topsail blew out. We spent nearly all
our free watch working at bending a fresh sail. It poured with rain that evening.
With the heavy seas and strong westerlies, we had to brace up square. Not a
very good day, and my wrist was painful now.

Injury or sickness at sea aboard a sailing ship was a calamity. For medical
assistance, sometimes for over a month, we depended entirely on the master's
medical knowledge, his medical manual and his medicine chest. Bad cuts,
bruises or clean fractures meant only light work and lookout duties. For anyone
to lie up in his bunk, the damage to the body had to be bad and obvious, or the
sickness easily diagnosed. There was no escape from any medical predicament
once under way even if several were stricken or injured. For with no radio to
obtain help and no chance of diverting to a near port unless lives were in serious
danger, one had to put up with the discomfort or pain of one's ailment. In the
lucky event of being taken off by a passing steamship, wages would be stopped
and there was no such thing as workers' compensation payments.

'Oscar', our last pig, was killed at this time. It was sad to see him depart. He
had become a familiar personality, snuffling around the deck, loose in good
weather and nosily pushing in to inspect what any of us was doing on 'his'
foredeck. He put up a great fight, knocking and tripping over a few, and it took
a good while to catch him. He was in the end dispatched with a blow on the
head with a maul and his throat cut. He was bled into a bucket the contents of
which were mixed with salt, flour and oats. This was then cooked in the oven
and we had fresh blood pudding for supper. The best parts of his carcass went
aft.

From now on we ran nearly square before the westerlies on an ESE course.
Our main work was changing all the sails from the fair weather set back to
heavy-duty storm canvas. So as not to lose any more sails, we were now
constantly reducing sail as the wind increased and then resetting the same again
as the wind's strength decreased. Most of the time we endeavoured to carry up
to our lower topgallants, even at times the upper ones. Our eagerness to make
port quickly now consoled us for having to climb up masts and out on the yards
throughout every watch.

About this time our invaluable donkey engine broke down and we were back
to hand pumping three hours a day. However I was then doing only light work,
nothing aloft and no trick at the helm as my wrist was still bad and inflamed.

The wind died away for a day and during this slack time the lads tried their
hand at catching albatrosses. Two of these magnificent birds were captured.

One had a wing span of nearly eleven feet. This old salt was very indignant at being hauled out of its element by lowly mortals. They were caught by trailing a metal triangle astern, one side of which was baited with meat. The bird goes for this meat, putting his upper beak through the triangle, and the line is quickly made taut. The bird inevitably pulls back, thus locking in its beak all the more and it is rudely pulled to the stern then up and onto the poop. They were measured, photos were taken, and the vessel's name was painted on their wings. Then they had a feed of tidbits that they snapped voraciously, biting at all their tormentors, and they were at last dropped back over the stern with much flapping of the big wings. After a long awkward effort they eventually took off and became airborne again to wander the southern oceans on the wing, where they have no equals.

On the next day a fair strong wind came away again from the west. As well as setting and furling sail, we were continuously bracing the yards to gain the maximum speed as we made for the Cape, and we averaged 7–8 knots on the starboard tack. The port watch took their shore clothes out for airing as we were getting towards port. The starboard watch, unfortunately, had now only their well-worn working clothes.

Two happy events occurred on this last lap. The donkey engine was tenderly overhauled and came back to life, saving us some hard labour. And the steward issued the contingency stores that he had had to keep aside in case our voyage was even further prolonged. These were tinned provisions that he did not want to keep now that he knew he would be able to obtain fresh supplies soon. Water was also taken off ration.

It was time to prepare the anchors for arrival, which was a labour-intensive operation on sailing ships. The crane was unlashed and lifted from its seating by a tackle rigged on the forestay, then lowered into its base socket housing. The cement cover of the spurling pipes was broken open, the plugs removed and the ends of the anchor cables lifted out of the lockers, also with the aid of hand tackles. On each side, we fed the chains over the gipsy* then through the hawse pipe. With the capstan, we paid out of the hawse pipes a length of chain sufficient to enable us to bring the coupling shackles up to the level of the catheads.

Both anchors were then unlashed from their deck cradle fittings, lifted by the crane and lowered over their respective side to their releasing position on the catheads. The slip chains were affixed, holding each anchor in position and allowing the crane to be unhooked. Then the cables were shackled onto each anchor and all was ready. All that was needed to drop the anchors was to release them by hitting a bolt pin after taking off the windlass's brakes.

About 200 miles off we were surrounded with Cape hens and mollymawks. At this time it was estimated that our compass was 4 points out, so it was with some relief that we sighted Table Mountain the next day. The sighting was a bit of an anti-climax to me. I expected to be a lot more excited. Naturally, we got a headwind which took us out of sight of our landmark for another day. But after much tacking and a favourable wind veer, we at last made Table Bay and dropped our anchor at 10pm on Saturday 22nd March 1947.

Up aloft we went, eyeing the shore lights which twinkled enticingly. With a satisfying feeling we furled our sails with a 'harbour stow', folding the leech in properly from the yardarm, tucking and rolling the whole sail right up onto the top of the yard with as few bulges in it as possible, fastening the gaskets evenly with no 'Irish pennants' (hanging rope ends).

A tug came out on Sunday morning but went away again. Our donkeyman had bargained a bottle of brandy from the captain for grooming his engine for the final effort of hoisting the anchor on time for the tug's arrival. Alas he drank it first and was incapable, or drunk enough to refuse, to start his engine at the time. He also resisted the mate touching it. So we got out the capstan bars, and after the chippy had reengaged the gipsy we trudged around the capstan all the morning till the anchor was shortened up.

Out came the tug again and this time we passed it a line. Soon the anchor was hove up and we were towed into the Duncan dock where quite a crowd had gathered to see us berth. Alongside at last we were able to clean up as best we could and finally go ashore, except for the watchman.

For paupers like Martin and me, unfortunately, there was not much choice of shore destination. It had to be the Seamen's Mission.

We had been 83 days out from Karlshamn, a voyage that normally would have taken less than half this time. But we were both proud to have experienced such a baptism on this first post-war voyage of the *Passat*.

Chapter 3

SOUTH AFRICA

Our passengers departed on arrival, including the three film crew from the UK who subsequently put together a documentary about the romantic voyage of a twentieth-century 'windjammer'. I saw it some years later and I thought 'If only the viewers knew the real story!'

All the passengers had had their fill of life on the 'briny' under sail, and they were down the gangway immediately. On the 83-day voyage the forecastle hands had had practically no contact with them. The one who most attracted attention was a younger woman who was travelling with her son aged about five years. She was, we were told, from England and was an artist. She used to paint with her board and easel around the deck in good weather.

There was also an elderly couple from Finland. The rumour was that the man was a military general who had held a high position in the Finnish security force during the war. It seemed a very unusual way for such an important person to leave his country.

The timber cargo was taken out by cranes, the dockers making up the slings in the hold. Roughly one third of our cargo was discharged in Cape Town which only took about two weeks. But our stay turned out to be an extended one of five weeks as we then had to wait for the dry dock to become free. Not the one in the Duncan dock complex, which was at that time the largest in the southern hemisphere, but the old Robinson dry dock.

We were finally shifted out of the Duncan dock and around to the old dock complex to make way for the visit of the future Queen of Great Britain. I am sure there was plenty of room just to shift us along the long wharf, but we might have detracted attention from HMS *Vanguard* on which the Royals were travelling and from their escorts. And, admittedly, our hull was still an unsightly rust colour not having had the chance of being treated yet.

The Royal visit affected us in as much as we had to 'dress' ship. We looked pretty smart with four hoists of flags flying from truck* to deck. I visited the *Vanguard* with Martin and we were quite impressed at her size and power.

During our stay in this port we were on day work five and a half days a week except when night watchman. We were employed at overhauling and renewing any worn running rigging and painting the top-coat over our preparations on the fore and after decks.

Eventually we were docked and our sprung plate was re-riveted in place. We went over the side on stages and painted the topsides black and the boot-topping green. The under hull was finished off after its 'haircut and shave' (chipping and scraping) with the usual red anti-fouling paint before coming out the dry dock.

Our main 'port of call' ashore was the Sailors' Society and the Seamen's Mission. I can say they were a most generous haven for us, even rigging us out with second-hand but good shore clothes.

A few of us were also invited out to the homes of people who had come aboard on Sunday visiting days and had befriended us. I got to know an English-speaking family from a suburb out past Observatory. They had a son a little younger than me and a daughter, who was very nice but unfortunately a little older and of course more mature than me. They were very generous, giving me an open welcome to their home if I wished. Some years later I visited them again when calling at Cape Town on another ship.

I went on a couple of occasions to the infamous nightspot the Del Monica. One night there we witnessed an all-in brawl between US navy sailors off a visiting warship and UK navy men off the *Vanguard*. It was a memorable spectacle, the fight spilling out onto the road amongst the traffic. The police pickets of both navies had to call assistance from the local constabulary to quell the hostilities.

The master, after consultation with the mate and sailmaker, had obtained permission from the Company to order several new sails, including three 'courses' (the large lower sails), to be cut out and made ashore. We did not have the time or really the space to make these before a possibly long and rough voyage immediately after discharging the last of our cargo. So the shore sail loft sent its foreman down to measure up with our sailmaker's help. None of the new sails were ready before we left so they were sent on to Durban.

By sailing day we were short of quite a few crew, some of whom were not prepared to sail any further under the conditions prevailing aboard, while others we knew had planned to start a new life in another country when they first joined in Finland. One of the two Swedish naval cadets returned home. The third mate 'got out': I cannot remember if he went officially or jumped ship. The second mate did jump ship, as did an AB and two deck-boys. The master was not happy to have to pay the fines to the authorities who would now put out search warrants for those who had so become illegal immigrants. The replacements were not too hard to get. The sailmaker was promoted to third mate and a South African second mate was signed on who had a square-rig ticket having done his time for such in the *Lawhill*. Another ex-*Lawhill* local AB and an OS were engaged, as well as three local deck-boys. Last but not least we gained another apprentice, Bob Deacon, whose father was the port's Harbour Master and wanted his son to experience sail as he had done himself when a lad.

Whilst in Cape Town I received a replacement set of a correspondence syllabus that I had purchased from a navigation school in Limehouse before leaving London. The originals had been destroyed when the forecastle was gutted. These papers were to be completed and returned to the school for marking. This was a four-year course intended to prepare the candidate for a certificate of the Board of Trade enabling him to sail as second mate.

The course was designed for the training of deck officers on British merchant ships, where the candidates were to be granted time off to study and receive tuition from a ship's mate. At the end of four years it was expected that they would attend the navigation school full time for a few months before sitting for the BOT examination.

Of course, no such help was available on this ship. There was no hope of even finding any place to study in peace. And I was daunted by the material contained in the first three months' papers, especially as far as mathematics was concerned. I never excelled in this subject. In fact I had only a rudimentary understanding of algebra and had never heard of trigonometry, the basis of the principles of navigation. In the face of all these difficulties, I did not undertake the task with much vigour. I attempted it, receiving fair marks in subjects other than mathematics or physics in the results I received back, but I gave up after a year, hoping to be able to cram the necessary knowledge in at a full-time school when I eventually returned home. In the meantime I would limit myself to practising with Martin and Terry some subjects such as the Rules of the Road and signalling.

The Finnish lads who wished to get certificates did not try to study on the ship either, but they knew that on return home they would be able to get jobs with companies, then when their apprenticeship time was in, go to navigation school and sit for their ticket.

At 10am on Tuesday 29th April, being again A1 seaworthy and with a full crew, we were towed a few miles from the breakwater of Cape Town harbour. An anchor had been dropped on arrival at the berth to assist in hauling us off the wharf when we left. It was now taken in and I went down the chain locker to stow the anchor chain. This was a strenuous and filthy job. The chain had to be flaked neatly so that it would come out the spurling pipe at the top of the locker without bunching into a knot and jamming when the anchor was dropped on the next occasion. Modern ships have self-stowing lockers.

Before the tug let go we had loosed all the topsails and sheeted them home, and most of our fore-and-afters were set. We then braced and set topgallants. By the time all the buntlines had been overhauled and we had squared up all lines, removed all traces of shore clutter and washed her down, we had been on deck thirteen hours straight, having to grab the 11am meal on the run. At 7.30pm the duty watches were at last set, and our watch was on to midnight.

The voyage up to Durban was pretty uneventful for us but was a harsh baptism for the new first-trippers, three of whom were seasick for the first few days and one till we reached Durban. We took nine days to reach Durban and encountered various winds. We were sometimes becalmed and sometimes hit a gale.

In one strong blow two sails split and we had to send them down and replacements up. The preservation of our sails was foremost in our captain's priorities. We were taking in sail as soon as the wind increased to any fair velocity, then setting the same again a while later. Good training for the new lads.

After passing East London we encountered bad cross seas. This was the effect of the easterly current that sweeps round the Cape from the Atlantic meeting the Agulhas current sweeping south-westerly down the lower East African coast. This caused heavy rolling and filled our well decks with seas over both gunwales. On the seventh day out we were forced to run before a SE gale and came dangerously onto the coast above Durban. It gave us however enough room to wear ship onto the opposite tack and bear off the land. The exercise took us half an hour to complete but the gale had been too strong to chance tacking. On Thursday 8th May, after again wearing ship, we came back on the coast in the morning just below Durban Bay.

Under shortened sail we took the tug's line and by 3pm were alongside and tied up at our berth, all squared up with a harbour stow of the sails on the yards.

It had been a short run from Cape Town but we were still glad to get ashore to see the city. Once again the young lads were restricted as to their entertainment by the lack of money but some of us visited the famous, or rather infamous, nightspot 'The Playhouse' on several occasions. The desirable ladies were of course way out of our affordability and we had to settle for a few drinks spread over many hours.

Along with other contenders I had a tattoo put on my forearm, which I felt at the time was obligatory for sailors. So I was marked for life and this mark was from then on recorded in all my identification papers. I really enjoyed this port and city, its tropical atmosphere, its wonderful golden beaches and the surf of the Indian Ocean. We went swimming as many times as we could get off.

The old standby, the Seamen's Mission, was again well frequented. One Sunday a number of us were taken out on the bus of the Sailors' Society to a picnic up into the hills. This was a welcome opportunity to see the country and the Zulu villages. I can remember swimming in a river and chewing sugar cane. In all a very enjoyable and memorable outing.

The *Viking* was also discharging at a berth a couple of miles away from us, and we visited her several times before we sailed. After the first visit I felt glad I had ended up on the *Passat*, even with all the setbacks we had experienced. I was proud to be on a vessel with a pedigree such as the famous Flying P Line and not on an ex training ship. I am sure all our crew had such thoughts. Seamen are generally loyal to their own and will find some reason to extol their ship's superiority, fact or fiction.

Our shore-made set of sails arrived from the Cape Town sail loft and we bent a topsail to see how it fitted and drew when full of wind. The head, foot, and leeches were almost correct in measurement. But the measuring and cutting of the cloths that fill in the sail from the edges in a 'mould' to accept, hold and spill the usual amount of wind had left a lot to be desired, resulting in ripples, sags and bulges. When we bent one of the courses at a later date the mistakes were still more pronounced. The defects were even obvious to the apprentices, so they must have sickened the master, mates and older hands. We would have to make do with them however.

After twelve days, our second consignment of cargo unloaded, more minor repairs effected and fresh water taken, we left Durban at 10am on 20th May, late autumn, for the short run down to East London, our final port of discharge. Our South African second mate paid off here and our temporary third mate returned to being sailmaker. In their place came the second and third mates from the *Viking* to join us.

This short run was also uneventful. On leaving I went aloft up the mizzen and let go all sail on this mast, staying up there to coil up the gaskets and overhaul the buntlines. We experienced several rain squalls which made visibility poor. We overshot our destination and had to wear ship to run out to sea again. At last, after tacking this time, we came in at the correct point to pick up the tug that was waiting for us and which proceeded to tow us up the Buffalo river to our berth on the town side. We tied up at 2pm on 22nd May, 52 hours out of Durban.

The usual squaring up was performed, then, as cranes were going to be used, we released the bottom ends of the forestays to clear access to the hatches. In order to give the cranes as much room to swing as possible we braced the yards out of their way and also cockbilled the course yards. All this took a long time and as we were mostly out of money very few went ashore that night. Within a week the last of the timber cargo was taken out of the hold and sand ballast was put in to give us stability before we took on our next cargo.

Whilst on the town side we had a look at East London, its shop windows and its entertainment. This was only a small city compared with the previous two and I thought it a bit drab once out of the few main thoroughfares. So the Seamen's Mission again became our regular destination ashore. In fact, except for the local cinema and an occasional spree at a pub on the occasions when we were solvent, it was to be our main shore destination for a long time to come.

After a week we were informed that no onward cargo to anywhere had been obtained and that no grain was presently available at a favourable freight rate from any of the Australian outports. So we were to lay up and await further orders. This meant finding the least expensive safe mooring, but also staying ready for sea at twenty-four hours' notice. As there were no really suitable local anchorages, we were shifted over to a disused wharf on the other side of the Buffalo river.

Our new berth was far from the town by road. We had a long walk up our side of the river to a main road and a bridge that crossed over to the town side, then another long walk along the river back down to the city which was situated roughly opposite us. It took about an hour to get to the city this way, so it was decided that we would provide our own ferry in the form of our pram dinghy which held about five people not counting the oarsman or sculler.

The latter was whoever was the night watchman, and we all got our turn at this thankless task. Anyone who wished to go ashore after work was taken over by the watchman. When they wanted to return they came to the steps of the town wharf and hailed the watchman who was supposed to be listening at all times for such a call and immediately go over the side into the dinghy and scull across the river to pick up the passenger or passengers.

It was alright when there were four or five to be ferried at a time, but frustrating when only one or two wished to be taken over, and then as you were halfway across a couple more arrived and bellowed out for their water 'taxi'. Sometimes those in the dinghy were primed up on liquor and ordered the watchman to proceed and come back later for the late arrivals. On eventually recrossing to pick up the latter, it was often abuse and sometimes more, depending on who was watchman on the night.

This exercise became difficult when the river was running at full current. It needed a strong arm and a good sense of direction allowance to make the other side without being swept either up or down the river past the destination. All this was of course exacerbated when the river was in flood or when it rained heavily or both. The job was detested by all.

During this lay-up in East London we were engaged in comprehensive rejuvenation work on our ship. On days of rain or strong wind, with the cargo out and a minimum of ballast in, we were put to work on cleaning out and painting the 'tweendeck and all that was accessible of the lower hold. The sailmaker, with the aid of some ABs, worked on new sails or on repairing old ones now that there was plenty of room in the 'tweendeck.

Our other job, and the main one, was the chipping, scraping, red-leading and painting of all the masts, yards and jib-boom. For this we first loosed all the sails on one mast and thoroughly dried them. They were then sent down and inspected for any repair needed. Those that were good were made up, lashed and stowed away; the others were sent down below deck for repair.

We then attacked this mast's yards with hammers, scrapers and paint brushes. Then, starting from the truck, we came down the mast doing the same. Then it was on to the next mast and so on, day after day, week after week. It was immensely boring, but we were kept on our toes by the hawk eyes of the mates who would inspect our handiwork for 'holidays' (unpainted spots) or unremoved rust. Whoever was the culprit went up again in his own time to re-do the missed parts.

When up aloft in the topgallant rigging we were above the adjacent cliff on the river bank, and here I watched every day other humans who were far worse off than us who were feeling hard done by. These were black prisoners in their hundreds who broke rocks in the compound at the top of the cliff. Seeing their conditions, their continuous demoralising task and the treatment dealt out by their guards, I truly felt sorry for all that were there whatever their crime, if any.

We were rather ignorant of social circumstances in South Africa, but since we had been there we had realised that there was a division of society between the Europeans and the native and mixed-race people. We had seen that whites had separate toilets, separate seats on buses, and that the others were not allowed to mingle at all with whites. At that time there was no actual law against inter-racial marriage, this came later with the ascendancy of the Afrikaans, but a few of us found out in this port that fraternisation between races was already under attack.

I and some other young lads had been seeing some coloured girls in the evenings when ashore. They were very attractive and quite shy. The lass I was keen on was not much darker of skin than myself. We never considered we were doing wrong or that it was any other persons' business.

Our illusion that we were in a free country was shattered when one night we were accosted by a carload of white men who ordered our girls to depart and told us, who were prepared to do battle over this intrusion, to leave black girls alone otherwise they would charge us with any crime that would fit.

They disclosed their identity as plain-clothes police and said they had had us under surveillance for a few nights. After a lecture on race purity they ordered us back on board. We had no choice but to comply and forget about our budding romances. That was the last time I went over the river, except to the mission. The insult has remained with me ever since and ensured that I never had any desire to live in such a country where a small minority lords it over the original people.

My only other interest in our long and now depressing stay at this port was a brief flirtation with the daughter of the owner of the small general store a thirty-minute walk along the river-bank road on our side.

*

With hindsight it is perhaps difficult to judge whether I was exceptionally partial to amorous delights at the time or whether I was already trying to fit into the mould of the traditional jolly sailor who has a girl in each port. As a matter of fact my younger shipmates all displayed the same rather obsessive interest, and our main pursuit when ashore was to try to pick up girls or imagine ways to obtain cheaply the favours of the glamorous ladies haunting the sailors' bars.

At sixteen I was by no means new to matters of sex. Indeed I am told that I was rather precocious in that respect, perhaps due to special circumstances of my childhood.

Like any normal boy, I was aware at an early age of the gender differences, and was very curious to know, learn and experience girls. When about seven I was caught playing 'naughty' games with the girl next door in their shed by her mother. The lass was, I think, a bit older than me. My parents were brought into this innocent incident but I only got a telling off and no hiding.

Curiosity grew with age and was eventually satisfied somewhat when I was evacuated with the school to the country at the outbreak of war. There, with no parental care, we got up to pastimes we would never have dared to contemplate at that age during normal times.

Quite a few girls from about 9 to 13 years entered into barter for their sexual favours, some losing their virginity first to inquisitive fingers, then later allowing boys to 'do' them as we called it. The price they asked from us was so many comic papers, the *Beano* or *Dandy* being the top of the currency. Depending on a girl's desire for comic literature we had the opportunity to be masturbated, orally stimulated or, if one had enough comics, to be able to go all the way, or as we called it to 'do it proper', staying in at climax.

By twelve years I had achieved the latter a few times. Neither boys nor girls gave any thought to the danger of pregnancy, in fact some of the boys did not even make the connection between sex and childbirth. We had never heard of venereal diseases. We knew about 'French letters', but they were only for grown-ups.

Most girls however on reaching full puberty and starting their periods ceased indulging in the comic-book sex market, and only under pressure from boyfriends allowed full intercourse to take place.

When I came back to London at the end of 1942, a girl in our street and I became sweethearts. I will call her Pamela. We made good use of bombed-out houses, and sometimes, if we found them unlocked, of air-raid shelters which were fitted with bunks and bedding. She only ever allowed me to stay in her all the way once. From then on I was made to pull out and if I did not I was pushed out. At other times we satisfied each other by hand or mouth. It was my darling Pamela who patiently taught me the art of using my lips and tongue on her clitoris to satisfy her. That was the extent of my sexual exploits until I went away to sea.

From then my only experiences were with the South African coloured girls just mentioned. With a few exceptions, these were mostly quick unromantic 'in and out' episodes, sometimes even standing up. This latter position was a very tiring one and had the apt title of a 'knee trembler'.

Pamela and I had parted like good friends some time before I left London for Mariehamn. Although I was fond of her I never thought of maintaining a permanent relationship with her, and neither did she apparently. However I received a letter from her while in South Africa. She had gone to see my father in order to obtain my mailing address. She expressed the wish to resume our relationship. I agreed but as this could now only be a correspondence affair I had no pang of conscience chasing other girls in the meantime.

In the event, this turned out to be a short-lived fancy on the part of Pamela. After a couple of letters from her, I had, even before leaving South Africa, a letter from her father informing me that his daughter did not wish to continue her relationship with me as she had found another lad who had better prospects for her. This came as a shock to me. At the time it probably hurt my pride rather more than it saddened me.

*

Far more disturbing for me was the news coming from home. I had received a letter from my father announcing that my 'terrible' mother had left him. Although I knew only too well that home was a very unhappy place owing to my father's tyrannical and brutal behaviour, I had never envisaged that such a thing could happen.

I no longer had a home to return to. I had the sickening feeling that my past was collapsing behind me. My father, in his letter, offered me a place to live in the future, but this was a laughable alternative considering our strained relationship. His way of charging all blame to my mother was anyway most offputting, as she had always been the most dedicated, tolerant and loving homekeeper.

Nevertheless I could not help feeling some resentment at her action, whilst at the same time being very worried about her own future, guessing that my father would certainly never give her anything to subsist on.

Naturally I craved a letter from her but I had to wait for that a good while. When it did come I was thankful to know that she was safe. She had gone to stay with my aunt Edith and grandmother and, although not in good health, at least was out of harm's way. She was herself sorry for me and apprehensive as to what my reaction would be and begged my forgiveness for breaking up the home.

I presently received a letter from my sister Joyce who gave me some details on the circumstances. She said that my mother had been putting up with hell for a long time (which I was well aware of) but that since my departure things had become much worse. Joyce eventually made Mum realise that to stay with this brutal husband any longer, just for the sake of maintaining a home until I moved on in life, would be as good as committing suicide.

One day after my father had left for work, Joyce came and helped my mother pack her possessions, and they left. According to the neighbours, when my father came home and understood that his slave had rebelled and escaped, he went berserk.

*

Over this two-month period we finished all the masts, yards and jib-boom, and our tophamper, now a shiny straw colour, certainly looked fine. Next we tackled all the standing rigging, whitening it down with white lead and tallow. We also replaced two port topmast backstays, a main topgallant forestay and the mizzen top forestay.

There were more crew changes here as all the South Africans except Bob Deacon had now signed off. As replacements two Germans who had been prisoners of war in South Africa joined us as ABs. They had found themselves on German steamships in South African ports at the declaration of hostilities and had been interned for the duration of the war. They then remained in the country but failed to settle, and so they were taking this opportunity to move on to Australia and see how they would fare there. Amandas Zimmerman who came into the starboard watch was from Hamburg. Kurt Schnell from Munich went into the port watch. Also joining us was another apprentice, Glen Ruck of Cape Town. We were again up to our complement.

Of the crew members who had absconded in Cape Town, the second mate and two Finnish deck-boys, Karl Teppo and I think Pekka Kouvenan, had been caught by the authorities and sent to East London's jail to be put aboard when we sailed. The two boys in the end were put in solitary confinement for twice trying to escape. When it was realised that our stay would be prolonged and a Norwegian vessel required replacements, the three were offered the jobs by the authorities, who were footing the cost of their keep, and they naturally accepted, the second mate signing as carpenter.

As our remaining Finnish deck-boys had now been on articles for a year they were promoted to *lättmatros*. Alas I and the other British boys were to be kept poor for a while yet as apprentices.

In the early part of our tedious wait for orders, hopes of a speedy departure had been raised when we had news that the *Viking* had sailed from Durban with coal for Buenos Aires and was then slated to load a cargo of grain from there for Europe. In fact, the latter cargo never eventuated and she finally sailed in ballast from Buenos Aires to Spencer Gulf where we met her later.

As for us, it was not until early August that we received the wonderful news that we were to proceed in ballast to Bunbury, West Australia, to load railway sleepers for Malaya. We jumped for joy to be getting to sea again and escaping our internment in East London, and all the first-trippers were thrilled at the prospect of going from our next port to the mysterious East Asia.

Supplementary sand ballast was loaded out of railway trucks that were shunted alongside until we had enough stiffening to make the voyage across the Indian Ocean in safety. When this was completed we laid shifting boards over the top of the sand and tied these down with wire and chain rove through rings positioned on the frames. This was to ensure that the ballast remained distributed evenly throughout the hold and did not shift if the wind or sea force heeled the vessel over.

We also bent the rest of our storm set of sail, ready for a Great Circle voyage that would take us down to the top of the Roaring Forties, that band of strong, constant westerly winds below 40° S which has been termed 'the sailing ships' highway'.

Chapter 4
ACROSS THE INDIAN OCEAN

At noon on Thursday 14th August we sailed from our berth and out of the Buffalo river with the assistance of a tug. On clearing and dropping the tug we set a course SE by E, and having a favourable but squally NW wind we set only topsails, main lower topgallant and foresail at first so as to test our stability. We had not even bent the royals. But we were soon logging eleven knots and were well on our way, glad to be back at sea at last.

Now that the Finnish lads had become OSs I picked up the job of lamp trimmer that 'Yanny', Hans Hongel, had jealously guarded over his first year. It was a responsible but easy, non-physical job, taking approximately two hours of each daylight watch. So I gladly exchanged my rigbag for those implements needed to illuminate our mobile floating home,

All lighting aboard was by kerosene lamps and these all had to be refilled, their glasses cleaned and wicks trimmed each day. Every cabin had a lamp, some had several. The most important ones were the navigation sidelights, the sternlight and the binnacle* lights. They all had spares, primed at the ready for emergencies. On a few occasions, we had a panic when, in heavy weather, the binnacle lights were extinguished. During the time it took to re-light the lamps or, if they were washed out, to light and insert the spares, the helmsmen on a black night had nothing to get a fix on so as to hold us more or less on course.

A welcome change for everyone was a great improvement in our menu. The steward's provisions had been replenished and the variety extended. We even had extras such as tinned evaporated milk, cream, jam and cheese, and we had fresh bread until it went too stale even to soak and re-heat. All this made our life a lot happier. Now that he had no passengers to cater for, the cook's task was easier, even though the saloon fare was still different from ours, and much better naturally.

As we were in ballast with little water on deck, we were kept employed at painting around the poop deck and the after well deck with white, grey, black and silver on gunwales, hatch coamings, bulkheads and machinery. We also cleaned out and painted the new lifeboat, purchased in Cape Town for 350 pounds to replace one of those lost in the Atlantic (the other lost boat was never replaced). Then onto the remaining lifeboat and the motorboat. This paint work, in addition to the sailing routine, kept us fully occupied well over twelve hours of each day and sometimes a good number of hours on our so-called day of rest, Sunday.

Alas our spirited start did not last for the wind dwindled and as we progressed SE we endured variable winds and at times were becalmed. For a week we had all sails set except the royals. Bracing from tack to tack was the order of the day. We were taking a long time to find the permanent westerlies.

I had a memorable encounter one day in these waters as I came out on deck during a free watch. Our toilets were forward under the forecastle head, so in fine weather and especially in ballast, if we only wished to urinate, we would step from our forecastle onto the foredeck, look for the lee side, climb onto the after well deck bitts, and relieve ourselves into the sea over the topgallant bulwark. That day, I proceeded at this function in a half-asleep condition and with the vessel nearly stationary and rolling slowly on the long swell. When about finished I focused my vision on a spectacle a few feet below me which, for a few seconds, frightened the hell out of me. Something huge was rising to the surface alongside. I about fell off the bitts in shock and amazement, but with effort controlled my balance and shouted my hardest, to anyone near at hand, to come and view the monster.

It was a whale, and a big one, as long as the foredeck. It had possibly come to inspect us as another large denizen of the deep. After rubbing itself on the hull in an affectionate manner and spouting a cloud of water vapour, it sank out of sight again. Once more it surfaced and blew, a ship's length off, as if to bid us farewell, and was not seen again. There was of course no more sleep for me that free watch after such excitement.

We at last hooked onto the real westerlies in Lat. 42° S. We squared away and ran E by S carrying most square sail, the fore-and-afters not being of much use with the wind right aft.

Martin, who had some knowledge of navigation, was able to work out our position each day from the knots we had logged, our course and allowances for magnetic deviation and variation. We were making exceptional progress for a vessel in ballast and were also receiving very little seas on deck. With such good circumstances and the safe trim we had, it was decided to send up, bend and set the royals. We were northing up to the edge of the westerlies again, and we had wind aplenty one day, then little the next. In such circumstances it is difficult to predict whether the voyage overall will be fast, slow or average.

On Sunday 24th August, I wrote in my daily log: '10 days out. Course E by N. Pos. Lon. 87 E, Lat. 42 S. Making a good run now. Averaged 13 knots over 24 hrs, 6 degrees approx 270 miles.' We were over halfway now and it seemed that we would make an average run port to port. By noon the following day the wind was petering out and our speed was markedly reduced. One man only was again needed at the wheel. The staysails were hauled up the stays, the tacks ready to be taken over, as the winds veered, to become the sheets.

At this time we had to start bailing out the bilges as a good few tons of water had accumulated, having drained from our sand ballast since it was loaded. Although pumping out the bilge meant a reduction in our total ballast, the presence of a large amount of free water slushing around the hull posed a greater danger as it would contribute to destabilise the vessel in the event of severe listing. We did this by hand for a few days by means of the main bilge pumps and by bailing. It was not till most of the water was out and we were only a few days out from port, that the donkey engine was put to use on this awful task. As soon as we were thus relieved, we went back to painting on deck.

*

Our Finnish shipmates had about accepted us as such at last. We were no longer the first-trippers and we had slightly better positions in the pecking order owing to the time we had served. And we were older. I was all of 17 years and, like the others, had developed in size, knowhow and strength.

Our new second and third mates had proved very acceptable. They were efficient and even appeared 'likeable' to the apprentices. This judgment was of course influenced by the fact that our competency at our jobs and our own confidence had increased after nearly a year aboard. There was hardly a task we could not handle and we were pretty proud of the fact.

As for the first mate, he always was a world apart from us. We knew he had a master's certificate in sail but to our knowledge he had never been in command. He only spoke to give orders, and then these were relayed through the third mate if possible. He was not a big man but he looked tough with his weather-beaten face made more noticeable by a scar on one side where one eye was missing. Whether he lost this in an accident or from a wound received in the war I never found out. I was very wary of him and treated him with great respect.

On the whole, we were a rather good forecastle bunch in both watches. Of course we 'Starboarders' considered ourselves the better watch.

The two German ABs who had joined in East London were proving a great asset to the work force, being top seamen and willing workers as well as good shipmates, although Amandas, who was well into his forties, had a short temper and often became impatient with us, young know-it-all upstarts.

One exception to the rough and tough but generally friendly harmony that prevailed on board was the conduct of one Finnish AB in our watch, who on occasions made life unpleasant for most and hell for some, including me. He was tolerated in general as he kept his own company, said little, was clean and, when sober, was a fair member of our fraternity to live with. But when drunk, he became a menace to all, upsetting the whole forecastle until he had sobered up. This did not happen while at sea, of course, since no liquor was allowed on board and drunkenness would have been severely dealt with by the officers. But it occurred in South Africa most times when he got paid and was able to get ashore to spend his money on drink.

When that came around, he would return at any time of the night and whether or not anyone was asleep, would crash into the forecastle shouting for all to get up and to join him. Even when no one responded he would keep up his racket not caring if we needed sleep. If we had the gramophone in our watch and he spied it, he would play records, often the same one over and over again. A few would try to remonstrate with him but he intimidated all and told them to go to hell.

He considered himself the top dog of the watch and as long as no one was bellicose enough to challenge this opinion of himself he enjoyed bullying others. He had got away with this conduct because, during our stay in South Africa, he was the senior to all of us, being the only AB left in our watch. I am sure that if the other two ABs who were originally in the watch had experienced this behaviour he would have been challenged. He was around forty years old, with a fair physique and a tough disposition, and most of us youngsters were wary of him. This character showed me once a folding wallet he had. On the inside of the fold he had pinned two Russian Red Army soldier's hat badges. He pointed to them and with a gleeful sneer drew his finger across his throat. I had been told that he had fought in the Finnish–Russian war and had been at one time a guard at a prisoner-of-war camp. Judging from his domineering attitude with us I had no difficulty believing that he had indeed cut their throats.

I made the mistake on one of these altercations of trying to appeal to his conscience by saying that he was depriving us of sleep when we had a hard day coming up, and that he should get the needed sleep also. He climbed on the bench seat, leaned over to my bunk and after pulling back the curtain punched me in the head. I shouted for him to cut it out and turned over to face the bulkhead but he grabbed my arm and twisted it up my back till I screamed out again with pain. He was enjoying this, saying that little boys never told him what to do, and that I was a nothing, only an English nobody.

At this moment a few of the Finns protested, one saying that he would be in big trouble if he hurt me and I could not work. This must have made him see sense, to my great relief, as he desisted and after abusing everyone again at last climbed in his bunk, proffered a parting tirade and fell asleep.

For the rest of the time he remained with us I kept well clear of him unless I had to work with him on a job. None were sorry when he jumped ship in Western Australia, in fact we were all relieved. This story shows how one unsociable individual can seriously upset forecastle life. Fortunately, except for a few minor incidents, none of my other shipmates disregarded the tacit code of the forecastle during my two years on the *Passat*.

The experience was another blow to my romantic expectations about seafaring but I took it as one of the knocks of life and learnt well from it.

Quite early after joining the *Passat* in Finland I had realised that life under sail was not going to be the magical experience one reads about in adventure books. My early enthusiasm was soon doused by the initial catastrophes suffered and the ensuing hard labour and rationing we endured. The reality was long hours of gut-busting work, acute fatigue, sleep deprivation, meagre and unpalatable meals, and cramped accommodation in damp forecastles.

The workload on sailing ships was always heavier than on other types of vessels. On steamships, except in exceptional circumstances, one has finished with work from the end of one's watch till the next. That is, unless overtime work is required, but then one is paid extra for overtime, usually at time-and-a-half rate and even double-time on a Sunday or in abnormal hours. Not so on a sailing ship. There was never overtime at sea. The vessel's safety, her sailing ability, as well as every life including your own, depended on giving freely your utmost effort at any time and almost to complete exhaustion.

In heavy weather, you often dreamed of taking a well-earned rest in your free watch, dry and warm in your bunk. But reality often prevented this, and one did not shirk being up aloft for hours fighting canvas, or armpit-deep in the well deck, watch-on or watch-off. That was your duty, and trying to evade it would have amounted to insubordination, with severe consequences, and would have furthermore exposed you to ridicule, scorn and even worse.

Such a life taught one the virtue of working in unity, of 'pulling together' (a phrase which no doubt was born on the decks of sailing ships). It showed that, in unison, men can master the elements, sometimes at great odds, and accomplish near-miraculous feats, such as driving 5,000 tons of ship and cargo by wind power alone around the globe. I only wished at the time that the remuneration for my effort would have been a little more generous. But at least I knew that our owner had done it all himself when young and was not, as some shipping company managers were, ignorant as to which end of a ship was which.

Along with my fellow apprentices, I often wondered if I had made the right choice. However as none of us had been deep sea before, we really had no point of comparison. We presumed that this was the normal life on most ships.

My brief previous experience on the *Serenity* had not been enthralling either. There the living quarters were warm and dry, and the food and the pay were better. But the workload was not lighter on the whole for me, 'the boy', than on the *Passat*, as I was at the beck and call of all even the cook and felt continuously picked upon. No sooner had we sailed from one port, than we were entering another, or going up some river, and I was called to turn out again.

From what our more experienced shipmates told us, life at sea was invariably gruelling, whatever the vessel. Kurt Schnell and Amandas Zimmermann, who had served in the Laeisz Flying P Line on either the *Priwall* or the *Padua* before the war, had experienced on these ships conditions as spartan as ours. These ships were run on a semi-naval style and were driven hard through all weathers. A significant difference in their case, however, was that the heavy workload was alleviated to a certain extent by the presence of twenty or more cadets who complemented a full well-trained normal crew.

On the other hand, some of the South Africans who had joined us in Cape Town, and subsequently signed off, had been able to tell us about the *Lawhill*, on which they had served on voyages such as the one we were now taking across the Indian Ocean. The South African government had fitted this vessel with a number of improvements which made the crew's life a little less primitive than ours. These included a radio transmitter, two extra fresh-water tanks (at the expense of valuable cargo capacity), a large ice-chest for fresh food, and hot water supplied by the donkey engine through piping, that allowed the whole crew to have showers and even steam baths at all times.

But we realised that this was an exceptional case and that the chances of securing a job on a subsidised vessel able to afford this level of amenities were few and far between. So, whilst knowing that life ashore could be more cosy, we all accepted the rigours of our present lot as inevitable. Life at sea was never going to be easy. Since we had chosen the seafaring profession, and were still keen on it, we had to steel ourselves to continue this grand adventure, and we derived some pride and satisfaction from our resoluteness.

*

As we came NE towards Australia we picked up favourable winds and kept them for the run up to our destination.

At this stage of the voyage we again enjoyed a slight improvement in our daily menu as we neared port in good time and the steward became able to apportion the remaining stores to the days left.

Thanks to my job as lamp trimmer, I had access to the lazaret store in the poop. When I was sure the steward would not surprise me, I sometimes managed to lift a tin of this or that from the back of unopened boxes of the delicacies that the forecastle hands did not see, and to get them forward undetected.

So, compared to our first voyage, this one was proving fine and we were mostly all happy with our existence, content to sail on into the future.

Soon the weather became milder and Martin, our 'navigator', told us we should start to keep our eyes alert when aloft for a sight of land. According to his reckoning, using the atlas lent by Terry from the other watch, we were in the vicinity of Cape Naturaliste, our landfall, at the lower point of Geographe Bay on which was situated the port of Bunbury, our destination.

Indeed, after the master and mate had worked out the position from the sights they had taken with their sextants at noon, the instruction was passed on down to us to keep a good lookout from aloft towards the starboard bow for a sight of land.

It was all magic to me that our old master could arrive so near our destination after the winds had blown us so far from a straight line between the two ports.

The navigation instruments carried on the *Passat* were those used by sailing masters over centuries. Although they were in principle able to provide quite accurate positioning when complemented with modern nautical tables and charts, in practice they gave only very approximate results, especially on board a sailing vessel, due to weather conditions, and navigation required great skill, experience and judgment.

There were three compasses on board. Two were steering compasses and these were placed near the two steering wheels, that is, one midships on the centre castle and the other right aft on the poop. They were positioned forward of the respective wheel at such a height as to allow easy reading by one or two helmsmen from either side.

These compasses were drastically affected by all the steel around them. Furthermore, this deviation varied constantly when the yards were braced around on different angles since these were all of steel themselves. The variation was less important for the poop compass which was further from the yards' influence and it would have been better from this point of view always to steer from aft, but as the *Passat* was a three-islander the steering was normally from midship where there was more protection from the elements.

The third compass was the standard navigation compass which was used to correct and check courses. It was also somewhat removed from the more serious magnetic interferences, being situated on a platform centred on the lifeboat skids high above the after well deck. This small platform deck was accessed from the after catwalk which ran on its starboard side. This compass was finely tuned and shielded with extra magnets to give the truest north as was possible.

Our position was determined from astronomical observations or estimated daily. When heavenly visibility was available the captain or the mate used a sextant to read the elevation of either a star at night or the sun by day and a pretty accurate position was calculated with the aid of nautical tables.

There were two chronometers, the second being a backup. Their function was to keep the Greenwich meridian time which is an essential component of the calculations. They were both adjusted daily on the noon Greenwich Mean Time signal that the master received on a battery-operated wireless receiver in his cabin, the only modern navigation aid on board.

But sometimes the heavens were overcast for days and it was necessary to use 'dead reckoning'. In this case, the distance travelled at noon since the previous noon was estimated from the log readings that day and layed out on the chart on the course that had been steered. All this was naturally guesswork to a large extent since the estimation of both the speed of the vessel and the exact course actually followed was very approximate.

To measure the speed we had the same primitive implement that had been in use for centuries over all oceans, the 'log'. It consisted of a wooden triangle with one side weighted so that it stood vertically on the sea's surface when being dragged along. It was joined to a line by a three-legged bridle affixed to the corners of the triangle. It was dropped over the poop rail and it floated astern as the vessel sailed away from it and the line was paid out. This logline was wound on a reel which a man held above his head. A sand glass was turned at the moment the log was dropped and when the sand had run through, the line was stopped and the point on the line read to the nearest mark.

The marks on the line were leather strips for the first three marks, then knots from then on, hence the use of 'knot' for 'sea-mile per hour'. They were spaced at 23ft 7ins, an odd figure for the layman, but in fact an ingenious way of allowing direct reading of the speed. The nautical mile being 6,080ft and the runtime of the sand glass traditionally fixed at fourteen seconds, at a speed of one mile per hour the log would pull out exactly 23ft 7ins of line in the time the sand ran out.

However the streaming of the log was never done on time methodically but only when the watch was free and able to carry out the exercise. So only an approximate run was ever recorded from this navigational aid, and in bad weather, normal in the high latitudes, streaming the log was very occasional.

The only other navigation aid was the 'lead line', used to measure the depth of the water. There were actually two of them. The hand lead line was used in shallow water, especially in rivers and channels, when it was necessary to ascertain the clearance of the vessel whilst under way. This lead was 'swung' by one man in the chains on the weather side and was to sound down to 20 fathoms (a fathom equals approximately 6ft, it is the span of a man's outstretched arms to fingertips).

The markings were as follows: 2F = two strips of leather, 3F = three strips of leather, 5F = white linen rag, 7F = red bunting rag, 10F = strip of leather with a hole in it, 13F = blue flannel rag, 15F = white linen rag again, 17F = red rag bunting again, 20F = cord with two knots in it. The in-between, i.e. 1, 4, 6, 8 and so on, were marked with a piece of marlin and were called 'deeps' when reporting the sounding. There were therefore nine marks and eleven deeps on a hand line. In the dark the leadsman obtained his reading of bottom depth by feeling the mark's substance.

The use of the hand lead line required some skill and strength as the operation was done at speed while the vessel could be travelling at a few knots. The linesman had to swing the lead (ours weighed approximately 8lb) as far ahead as possible so that it would touch bottom by the time he passed over it.

But the main lead line, as far as navigation was concerned, was the deep sea one. This was used at times when the results of the other checks on the vessels position were vague. Over the last two centuries oceanographers using soundings had mapped the hill and valley contours of the oceans' floor and recorded them on the charts. So when there was a range of submarine mountains marked on the chart with the nature of the bottom also mentioned (sand, mud, rock, shell coral, etc.) one could gain precious clues as to the vessel's position by dropping the lead.

This deep sea lead weighed 30lb. In order to pick up sample material from the bottom, it was 'armed' with tallow which was packed into a cavity in its base. On the old deep-sea lead the line was marked the same way as the shallow lead line down to 20 fathoms. Then the markings were knots corresponding to depths of tens of fathoms down to 120F, the full length of the line. At each 5-fathom depth between the 10-fathom markings was a single knot halfway mark.

This backup aid was in fact seldom used. The vessel had to be stopped in the water, so unless we were in an unusual calm it was necessary to heave to by backing the yards on a mast, a risky manoeuvre in heavy weather.

We carried a second, more modern deep-sea lead line which was coiled on a reel in a stand and was stored in the chart room. It had a lead roller to fit on the sheer strake* plate and take the line clear of the ship's side. It also had a brake and a reel handle to rewind the line.

Given the innumerable causes for error in the use of these instruments and the fact that for long periods of heavy weather none of them could be used at all, it was amazing that masters sailed often a lifetime of successful voyages with few casualties.

Of course our Old Man had been practising this 'magic' for a lifetime and had learned the skills from his tutors and from the experience of handling many a sailing vessel on such a run long before I was born. My admiration for his position grew considerably even though we never ever knew his thoughts as he kept, being in command, so aloof from us.

*

There was no free watch for us on this day of expected arrival. Land was sighted at breakfast time by the lookout who had been sent aloft for this purpose. Cape Naturaliste light had been observed long beforehand. Soon a reef was in sight about half a mile ahead. We braced as hard as we could onto the backstays and passed the reef with but a cable to spare.

We engaged in the usual preparations, lifting the anchors off their seats on the forecastle head with the anchor crane, swinging them out to the catheads, shackling them onto their respective cables that we had got up from the lockers. They were then ready for use in moments if necessary.

Both watches were engaged in shortening down. First the royals came in, then the upper topgallants, gaff topsail, crossjack and flying jib. By now we were well inside Geographe Bay. We spelled each other to have our lunch. The port watch went below, but after an hour, at 3.30pm, all hands were called and we sailed right up to and around Bunbury's breakwater, hove to, and dropped an anchor. When lying safely at anchor we furled the remaining sails, and braced up the yards, then squared up the deck 'shipshape in the Bristol fashion'. We then prepared the hatches, and we at last went below after fourteen hours on deck and 21 days out from East London.

Next morning the local tug, which was shared between Bunbury and Bussleton, arrived up from the latter port a few miles to the south. After the usual suspenseful performance of starting the donkey engine, we hove up the anchor and were towed up to the long wooden jetty. We ran a line out aft to the shore and the tug put us alongside.

Chapter 5

AUSTRALIA'S GOLDEN WEST

Bunbury was the centre of the farming area of the south-west of the state of Western Australia and exported mainly grain. But it was also the outlet for timber from the forests of this region, and especially for jarrah wood. This is an exceptionally durable timber as it gives off a particular sap which prevents decay and is repugnant to termites and other wood-eating insects. It is then ideal for railway sleepers in tropical conditions. Malaya had ordered a whole shipload of these sleepers to repair its run-down rail track.

Bunbury at that time had a very long wooden jetty which could berth four ocean-going ships safely. There were also to my memory four luffing cranes. The jetty was serviced by rail lines, so cargo could be delivered right up to each wharf or unloaded directly in rail wagons.

Our first job was to discharge some of our ballast so as to make room for the first slings of sleepers. The usual bracing of yards was done at the hatch that was to be worked first. The shore-side braces were slacked and cleared as were those forestays that would impede the crane and its grab dipping in and out the hatch. The ballast was carted away in the rail wagons and was probably sold.

Then the first consignment of sleepers arrived alongside on flat-top wagons. All the loading was done by waterside workers, locally known as 'lumpers' (although the more general Australian term is 'wharfies'). Two of them worked on the wagon making up and slinging about twenty sleepers for each hoist by the crane. Another guided the hoist down the hatch by signals to the crane driver. Twelve more lumpers worked in the hold, breaking the slings as they landed and stowing the sleepers neatly fore-and-aft in rows. They worked off a stack in the centre of the hatch under the crane's hook, sliding the sleepers out to the wings of the hold where each one was placed by two lumpers.

The men worked in to the stack until one layer was completed. When placing the following layer, the butt ends of the sleepers were staggered with the ones underneath, like bricks in a wall. This interlocking ensured that the pieces would not shift when the vessel was in seas that would throw her around. The last and top layer, unless fitting tightly under either the 'tweendeck head or the main deckhead, would be tied down with chain or wire lashings.

As the stevedoring company was contracted to work day shift only, the loading took a long time. The work was interrupted several times by spells of heavy rain and by the need to discharge more ballast as the cargo gradually stiffened the vessel, including the 800 tons of Finnish granite that had been stowed on the ceiling of the lower hold for years and that was sold to the port authorities. At times the lumpers also had to wait for the wagons to come from the timber mill. Then on a few occasions we lost the crane to another ship which took priority over us. So in all we were six weeks in port and about five weeks loading.

The crew did not mind this stay in port since this time we knew where we were going and had no worries about our immediate future. For us it was time well spent. Again, except for our meagre pay-day nights or an occasional Saturday night, the destination ashore was the Seamen's Club in the town. The minister in charge was very good to us and organised Sunday picnics followed by dances at night. The local girls were well represented at all these events. But naturally they were strictly watched over by the minister and his helpers, mainly older citizens. So none of us achieved any more in our courting than a kiss or two, and at the extreme, a longing feel of the forbidden parts of a more amenable and daring lassie's trembling body.

We found this very frustrating. We reckoned that if girls were supplied for the entertainment of sex-starved young seamen then such a prudish charade was a cruel joke. Of course, such is the practice at all the seamen's 'homes' and 'clubs' around the world. The seafarers who lack the finances to satisfy their desires at other venues can expect to be treated there with great hospitality, but the upright citizens who host them see to it that they are kept out of sin's way! This is inevitable for if ever one of these clubs relaxed its strict moralistic policy that would make headlines in newspapers and possibly result in the closure of these havens for poor seafarers.

The sex life of seamen is a source of endless jokes. It tends to be viewed with amused condescendence or with a sense of moral condemnation, sometimes by the same persons depending on their mood. But it must be realised that the long periods of chastity, and even total deprivation of innocent everyday female presence, imposed by life at sea (and this was worse in sail with voyages often taking three to six months) and the brevity of the sojourns on land are not conducive to sentimentality and restraint. On the contrary they can only generate obsessive frustration. To expect otherwise is totally unrealistic.

This is why the hospitality of the Seamen's Societies in all our ports of call, although thankfully appreciated, was far from sufficient to assuage our most pressing desires.

Prostitution thrives in all sea ports, to the shame and outcry of the god-fearing citizens, and it will continue to thrive whether it is legalised, tolerated or banned. I believe this profession has a quite legitimate social function. There will always be a section of society that cannot achieve fulfilment of their natural desires owing to their inability to find a partner at the only time they are available.

To condemn prostitution on the grounds that it exploits women or that it is a hotbed of anti-social activities is short-sighted. The men who use the services of prostitutes do not exploit women. They engage in a natural act for a negotiated fee. The women do not exploit the men. They make a living as they would do in any other profession. All this is perfectly honest. The real exploiters of this situation are the pimp, the brothel owner and their 'protectors', and the authorities themselves. It is repression that turns sex into a forbidden commodity paying immense profits and generating criminality and corruption.

The alternative was the so-called 'good-time girls' willing to drop convention and go with a stranger that took their fancy. They were generally lonely women craving for male company. They were prepared to engage in sex play even amongst open company by overcoming their inhibitions with alcohol. Many had had unhappy experiences with men. Some had been jilted whilst others had no chance of attracting a man under normal circumstances owing to their figure or looks. In an atmosphere of alcoholic revelry these women could achieve equality and sometimes satisfaction.

On occasions such women married seamen and were true and good wives but some, naturally, realising that their roving partner was possibly bedding another good-time girl in another port, entertained other seafarers when their own were away on long voyages. Some married seamen, quite naturally too, are hypocritical, and although they indulge themselves with this type of women when away, they have been careful to marry a woman living far away from any docklands and having no contact with other sailors' wives, whose exploits they might be tempted to emulate!

Given the choice, I am sure most seamen would prefer the company of a 'nice' girl to that of a professional or a frustrated loose woman. But the chances of meeting one who would accept to offer sexual gratification in the short time that a ship stayed in port and without commitment to a long-term relationship were negligible. In our younger years we often dreamed of it but that was sheer fantasy.

At this stage of my voyages, I already understood that these were the hard realities of the seaman's lot, as far as love and sex were concerned.

One change from our somewhat austere existence came with the arrival in port of the *River Murray*, a nationally manned vessel run by the Australian government. She was a large steamship for that era, a three-island vessel of about 6,000 tons with four hatches and about sixteen derricks. A few of us were invited aboard in reciprocation of most of her crew visiting us on many occasions. We were shown over their ship and were very impressed with their living conditions, wages and leave allowances, which were all better than the lot of British seamen and far better than those on Finnish ships. In comparison to our life it sounded like sailing on the good ship *Paradise*. I was invited to their noonday meal and enjoyed three courses of delectable food including roast beef and even ice cream with the dessert.

A few of us were also invited up the town on the Saturday night by some of their lads. They insisted they were 'shouting' us (paying for us), and we had a rip-roaring time at seeing the other side of Bunbury's social entertainment, including most of the pubs. The star attraction on that night was a dance in the lounge of a hotel in the centre of town the name of which I cannot recall.

Another interesting vessel to berth near us was the beautiful New Zealand topsail schooner *Huia*. We also visited each other and made comparisons. This vessel had made the fastest run across the Tasman under sail (a record that has not been broken since). She had an engine but had not had to use it on that passage.

*

My main interlude of our stay in this port was a trip to Perth, the capital of Western Australia. My mother had written to her brother Dick, the ex-mariner who had settled in this State, to tell him of my visit to Bunbury. One day I received an unexpected letter from this uncle of mine whom I knew only by hearsay. He invited me to come up to Perth for a few days to meet him and his family. He must have realised the financial plight I endured having experienced the same when he first went to sea, and he said that if I could raise the train fare to Perth he would pay the return fare. He would give my captain the guarantee of his word that he would put me on the return train on the day nominated. I was to show the letter to our master and let my uncle know the decision and my arrival time at Perth station if I was allowed leave.

I received six days' leave and a sub on my paltry wages to buy my fare. Apparently old Captain Haggerstrand trusted my uncle's word and had no fear of having to pay fines for my desertion. So after sending a wire to announce my arrival time I boarded the train the next day.

The train I took was known as the 'milk train'. It departed in the late afternoon, travelling overnight and stopping at many sidings to pick up fresh milk from dairy farms, and occasionally other goods, for delivery to Perth the next day. The distance was not great, approximately 110 miles, but owing to the frequent stops the train did not arrive till after 9am. Naturally, in the night I saw little of the countryside I was travelling through. Neither did I get much sleep on the hard seats.

My uncle and his wife met me off the train and my dishevelled appearance cannot have impressed them much. After formal greetings we boarded his big (to me) American-made car and off they took me to their comfortable timber home near the further bank of the Swan river in the suburb of Rivervale.

That evening I met my cousins when they came home from work or school. I forget how many there were, at least two boys and two girls I am sure. Next day my uncle and aunt took me into Perth and first put me in a barber's shop to get a proper shoreside haircut. I was then taken to the men's clothing department of a large store called 'Boans' where they fitted me out with a sports coat and trousers, then shoes and a shirt. Uncle Dick would not hear of repayment for the expense as he knew I would not have much money and would not wish to spend it on such luxuries as clothes. He said the pleasure of having a decent-looking relative to show around rather than a down-and-out young pirate was enough repayment.

The next few days were wonderful and I was well indulged, with kindness. On the weekend they took me on a picnic into the countryside to see the celebrated Western Australian wild flowers at their full bloom. It was indeed a marvellous spectacle with glorious colours stretching to the 360 degrees of horizon.

On the Sunday we all went to the beach at Scarborough, a magnificent expanse of white sand about twelve miles NNW of Perth. The beach stretched from the esplanade road to the water's edge and was very wide even at high tide. There was great fun for us youngsters, riding or attempting to ride the big surf breakers rolling in continuously from the vast Indian Ocean.

Alas the weekend was soon over. However my uncle and aunt took me on the Monday for a trip on the Swan river and to the zoo and King's Park which, I recollect, contained an interesting botanical garden. The Tuesday was simply spent in idyllic idleness. The next day was my departure on my trip back to reality.

I asked my uncle if he would come down to Bunbury to see my ship before we sailed. But he said that he had seen all he ever wanted to of sailing ships. A reply I could not understand at all. I felt a bit let down by my seafaring hero.

The trip back was uneventful and only took a few hours, but it was interesting. As it was by day, I was able to watch the passing countryside for the whole 100 miles or so, and realise the vastness of the continent.

*

After a few more days of topping up the 'tweendeck with sleepers we were down to our marks and all but ready to clear and depart the port.

We had been for a while overhauling gear aloft. The last few days prior to sailing were spent sending up and bending sails. As it was spring in the southern hemisphere we bent our middle set of sails which had been inspected and repaired as was usual when one was in port and the sails were down. Then it was batten down the hatches with the usual layer of thick timber lengths bolted down over the three tarps on each hatch.

There had been some changes in the crew at this port. Our sailmaker Ellis Elloma and our cook jumped ship. One of the South Africans, Glen Ruck, signed off and returned to Cape Town. Mike Ruffhead from the UK joined as OS (he had a second mate ticket) and another German, Dick Wallander, an ex-POW, also joined as an OS (he had been an AB on a German merchant ship interned during the war). Another cook was signed on as second cook. He did not stay long with us and I have forgotten his name. Magnas Lindvall, our original second cook, went first cook. Only eight of the initial twenty forecastle hands now remained. As well as our full crew we had some temporary supernumeraries: two pigs and eleven chickens.

On sailing day I was only just short of being one year on articles and so, like the Finns, wanted to become an OS, not only for the rank but in order to earn a lot more money than our miserly few shilling a week. However the master turned my request down, saying that we from the UK had signed on as apprentices at the stated rate of pay and would remain in that category till we signed off. So I had to do at least the next voyage to Malaya and wait till our return to Australia before taking up the matter again.

My visit to my uncle in Perth had caused me to reflect on the unexpected turns a life can take, and to muse about my own future. Here was a relative of mine who had cut himself off from his past and home and had reared a family in a new land on the other side of the globe. I had seen him happy and content with life. He had done well and was living in comfort, and he had apparently never been homesick. From the little I had seen of the country, I could glean even at that age that life was more fulfilling here than in old England. Even the climate made such a difference.

I never saw uncle Dick or his family again and I learnt a few years later from my mother, who had always kept in touch with her elder brother, that he had died.

Departure day arrived but we waited another 23 hours for a favourable wind to allow us to clear the bay and gain sea room without the help of a tug, a financial saving to the credit of our master. Mooring lines were let go, and with the power of the wind in sails that we had already set and sheeted home, *Passat* fell off the jetty. We squared the yards to advantage and steered her straight out to sea and deep water. More sail was put on up to upper topgallants and by dusk we were running heavenly and shipping heavy seas as she was down to her marks with her full cargo.

For the next ten days we headed mainly NW with a fair wind which, after passing the latitude of Capricorn, blended in with the SE trades. We headed out into the Indian Ocean to pass east of the Cocos Islands, then between the north tip of Sumatra and the Nicobar Isles, then into the Andaman Sea and down the Malacca Straits to our destination at the mouth of the Kelang river, halfway down the west coast of the Malay Peninsula.

Gradually the temperature rose and we were soon basking in tropical sunshine each day under a full press of canvas. Our work was routine during this period as little time was spent bracing or making and reducing sail. So again three men from each watch were put on day work, mainly making new sails and trying to alter where possible the ill-fitting set from Cape Town.

Again I stayed watch-keeping on account of my unacceptable left-handed sewing. However I was allowed to repair old sails and did a lot of this during the daylight watches. On one occasion at this time, when we were bending the old set of sails for the tropics, I lost my cap overboard. I was very upset by this loss, but not as much as Heiki, one of the Finnish lads, who lost his watch when the band broke.

This was turning out to be a happy voyage. Even the food had improved with the new cook. Sometimes we played the gramophone on No. 2 hatch while doing make and mend. In the free watches men occupied themselves at their favourite handicrafts. I made a pair of rope-soled canvas shoes.

We also took advantage of the fair weather to spend a good deal of time at gymnastics. The Finns, like all Scandinavians, and like the Germans and Russians I might add, are keen on physical exercise which is for them an important part of everyday life and not only reserved for professional competition. In their countries, much emphasis is placed at school on physical education.

Quite serious gymnastic training could be provided with simple equipment on the limited space of a ship's deck. On the starboard side of the foredeck was fitted a metal bar from the catwalk across to a backstay. It had a diameter suited to the average handgrip. It was at a such a height that you had to jump high to grasp it, and those small of stature had to be lifted up to reach it. There were also Roman rings, also hung from a backstay, and also at a fair height. The exercises that were performed on both apparatuses were those used in Olympic competition.

I had had some training at the bar when at school in England, but my abilities were at first miserable compared to the skill and muscular strength of the Swedes and Finns. Some were of exhibition standard.

Most of us became proficient to varying degrees. I do not think that any safety net was used and it was amazing that none of us broke any bones when trying to imitate the acrobatics of our Scandinavian shipmates and crashing to the hard deck after missing a grip.

Of course, it was only in long periods of fair weather, when the crew was not worn out with fatigue and when the vessel was on a near even keel and not rolling, that this pastime could be indulged in.

One dubious necessity to detract from the good life was that we were put on short water rations as our master reckoned that the water in Malaya might not be fit to drink. To exacerbate this crisis, dead rats were found in the after freshwater tank, meaning that only the forward one was now available for drinking water. Until we made port and found the water there perfectly safe, the ration was two quarts per day per man for washing as well as drinking. So back to seawater baths.

A few steamers were sighted during this time but only one passed close. We tried to speak to her by Morse code with our torch but she could not understand us.

We saw plenty of porpoises on this run, and also frigates which fly far out to sea. These birds have a large wing span, a short body, a long beak, hooked at the end, and a long forked tail. They are fierce and will kill and eat other birds.

At last the trade winds petered out and for a few days we were becalmed and endured countless rain squalls, none unfortunately lasting long enough for us to catch the quantity of fresh water needed to supplement our ration to any meaningful degree. A few of us swam over the side when becalmed, Anti Pojhula doing spectacular dives from the foreyard. We also rigged a canvas pool on the foredeck, so at any time we could jump into that and cool off.

Soon we picked up the monsoon winds usual for that time of the year. They were filled with rain squalls and many water spouts. We passed once through a line of fourteen of these, luckily evading all. I hate to think what damage would have been made to our fair weather canvas had we made an encounter. Quite a few land birds resembling hawks landed on deck for a rest.

At three weeks out we were off Sumatra having sighted, to the NW, presumably the Nicobar group. As the glass was falling we took in the royals and stood by in case of any sudden typhoons.

On 8th November at 6am we sighted the north-west head of Sumatra and by noon we were abreast of the Island of Pualo. Here we saw quite a few steamships, and also motorised junks and sailing praus. So we took in the mainsail and cro'jack so as to be able to manoeuvre better in any navigational emergency. At this point the wind failed us and left us drifting in the current which fortunately was going the right way. We hoped to make enough easting to be able to pass close by the Island of Penang so as to signal for a tug to meet us off Port Swettenham.

For the next two days we encountered light variable breezes, some but cat's-paws. Rain squalls were continuous and at least we were able to replenish our water supply and come off the ration. A large amount of flotsam floated by, branches and even whole trees. One of these drifting trees even harboured a fair-sized snake. We were constantly taking in sail, setting it again, tacking, whilst all the time being pushed down the Strait by the current. Junks, either under sail or motorised, were numerous. Some overhauled us, while others were beating against the current going the opposite way.

One night we passed a steamship and tried to signal her, Martin again using a torch. Alas she did not seem to make us out and she was soon out of sight. This was very frustrating. However we apparently had at last some success with another ship. We could not decipher her name. She may have been Greek or Russian. After half-guessing fourteen letters in the name we gave up. They must have read Martin and reported us, as the tug was alerted to meet us off our destination. Otherwise we could have overshot our destination as we were unable to get anywhere near to Penang to give our position.

At last we passed the islands of Kuala Perak far out on the port beam and were able to fix our position and to know we only had 150 or so miles to go, that is, if we were met by a tug or could anchor.

All this time, when not sailing the vessel, we had been oiling our wire towing and mooring cables on the foredeck and poop, taking great care not to stain our bleached wooden decking. This task had been very difficult, especially having to work in between rain squalls and to drop the job when the whistle went for our services at the braces or up aloft.

Gradually we paralleled our course further in towards the coast where we could see thick jungle interspersed now and then with a cluster of village buildings, many erected off the shore and over the water. At last the hoped-for tug appeared on the horizon. We were soon shortened down and when the tug was in position forward, after putting the pilot and agent aboard, we passed it our towing line on the end of a heaving line and we were soon under tow around the headland to our anchorage off Port Swettenham.

Chapter 6

AN ORIENTAL INTERLUDE

We anchored about a mile off a small craft jetty which was erected out from the shore. Port Swettenham, in the state of Selangor, was only a very small and minor port at that time. It was situated centrally on the west coast of the peninsula, at the mouth of Kelong river. The small town of Klang was a few miles up river, and a further 16 miles inland was Kuala Lumpur, the capital and British administrative centre of all the Malay States. Because of this privileged situation Port Swettenham later developed into a busy container port now known as Port Klang.

However in 1947 all ships loading and discharging did so out in the stream from barges and lighters and with the use of their own gear. While we were there, the first wharf berth was opened. It was located around to the south of the river mouth and was a prominent sight at night, being all lit up with floodlights for round-the-clock operations. I think it was an American President Line ship that was first in to use it. Many nations' ships called there, the majority however were British with Blue Funnel ones the most regular.

By the early morning after arrival day, we already had our yards trimmed and the hatches to be worked ready for cargo, and at 8am out came the first two lighters and two large gangs of dockers to start the discharge of our cargo of railway sleepers. Apparently we were only to work daylight hours owing to inadequate light after dusk. In fact the Malay railways department was not in a great hurry for the delivery. As for us, we also had plenty of time to spare as we did not have to be back in Australia until the new grain crop was harvested, bagged and ready for export. So being young, used to living from day to day and not inclined to hasten into the future, we were quite happy to enjoy a long stay in this exotic part of the world.

A roster was drawn up for night watchman, for motorboat coxswain (the motorboat was used for shore leave after work, and for the master, the agent or other official visitors at any time) and for cargo work. I explain in Appendix 2 the method we used to unload to lighters alongside. It required the assistance of three men from our crew at each working hatch. The most envied of these jobs was cargo tallying. This consisted of counting the number of slings discharged and the number of sleepers in each sling. The stevedoring company had their own tally clerks who sat next to ours. This was customary practice and it ensured there was no deceit causing loss of money to either party. Another man drove the winch and the third worked the yardarm nok* wire. The least pleasant of these rostered jobs was the handling of the nok wire which became worn and full of barbs. However we changed around during the shift and nobody spent more than three hours on the wire.

Thus when both hatches worked, six of us were required for cargo work. We actually all looked forward to our roster days because we received extra pay for cargo work from the stevedoring company. This was a most welcome addition to our pitiful weekly pay. The extra wage was equal to that paid to the Malay dockers, not very much, but to us it was a fortune and it made our stay in this port a memorable one.

The jetty where we landed when coming ashore was in the form of a T, with the cross of the T a floating pontoon reached from the shore across a wide wooden gangway. On the shore side of this gangway was a large timbered floor area under a roof. Inside this area and around the sides, hawkers had their stalls and wares. Sampans and praus were constantly berthing and leaving, filled with Malays, Chinese and Indians commuting to their hamlets around the river's mouth.

Originally the area had been a fishing and trading community, with hamlets built out over the water, of which quite a few remained. Water transport had been the only way to commute before roads were constructed through the jungle ashore, and still was for most. The jetty was therefore the focal point of the port and was always full of people, including those from or going to ships anchored off. Lighters and barges were loaded and discharged from small wharves and jetties further up the river.

From the jetty area one stepped out onto the main road which ran straight inland for over half a mile before bending and running roughly parallel to the river and continuing up to Klang township. The first part of the main road was like a high street with shops on both sides. There were bazaars, traditional Malay dance parks well patronised every night by the locals. There were also some other parks and an open-air cinema. This main road was surfaced, but the few cross roads were only surfaced for a short way in either direction. All was green, lush with vegetation, and the smells of spices, coconut oil and copra wafted prominently in the air. Tropical fruit trees abounded all about, even down the centre of the highroad. A bus ran to and from Klang where was situated the local government buildings, schools and a hospital. On occasions we ventured up to Klang but I found that the port supplied all the life and entertainment I could wish for.

One Sunday, early in our stay, I did venture further. I borrowed a bicycle and rode it to Kuala Lumpur and back. It turned out to be a long ride in the heat. But the road was excellent. It ran through rubber plantations and stretches of jungle where I saw lots of monkeys and many tropical and colourful birds. With a few rests at the tops of hills my excursion was uneventful and I covered the distance in good time. I rode around the city and had a look at its grand colonial buildings especially the stately railway station. After a cool drink I returned to the port pleased to have seen something of Malaya's inland.

The Chinese seemed to constitute about half the population. They were the entrepreneurs of commerce and the main owners of shops. There were a few Indian businesses but most Indians were in government jobs, especially the police force which counted a fair number of Sikhs. As for the Malays, they mostly kept to working their small farms. That is, the women did. The men, we observed, seemed to walk and sit around together all day.

I was befriended by a Chinese shopkeeper. He had a wife, a small son about eight years old, an elder daughter of sixteen years, who was very quiet as decorum required at that age in a girl entering the marriage market, and a younger daughter of about eleven who was a regular extrovert with sparkling eyes and always a smile. He also had two male student lodgers in their late teens. These were firebrands politically and very anti-colonial. We drank tea and discussed politics on a number of occasions. The shopkeeper did not participate in these debates but conversed mainly about business and enquired about life in England and Europe.

They all came out to visit the ship one Sunday. I felt that their sympathy for me was not entirely disinterested, but partly motivated by the desire to cultivate a business relationship. Not that I spent much money at their shop at that time, but who knows? I might return there on later voyages. Nevertheless I was happy with the acquaintance as they were all interesting individuals. I was especially honoured when I was their guest at a special meal cooked for the occasion by the shopkeeper's wife, who prepared several dishes on an open cooker in their little courtyard.

*

Meanwhile, I had developed in this port another interest than drinking tea and discussing the price of rice, and this concerned young persons of the opposite gender who could to some degree assuage my sexual appetites. This yearning was somewhat satisfied by a marvellous encounter which unfortunately ended in sorrow and shame.

Early during our stay, when coming ashore on a pay night, some of us lads were asked if we would like the company of nice young girls for a 'short time'. The fact that we had money on this occasion must have been 'telegraphed' ashore ahead of us. Nodding our consent to the young fellow who made the offer, we followed him to a Chinese settlement about a mile from the jetty and

then up a side road where we entered a house. We were sat down and given cold drinks by an older woman and a younger girl. Then we had paraded for us half-a-dozen young women looking shy and giggling. A few of the boys picked out ones that appealed to them and off they were taken to other rooms or houses after paying a bargained fee. I am certain the amount we had been paid had also been divulged to the madam as it fitted near to the amount she charged.

The younger girl, who turned out to be the houseowner's daughter, spoke good English and was the interpreter in all the introductions and price negotiations. It also became obvious, and was later confirmed, that the young fellow that had met us at the jetty was the madam's son. The other women and the madam herself only spoke a few words of English and chatted away in their own dialect, possibly Cantonese.

As I sat there I became fascinated by the daughter. She was simply beautiful. She was the only one I wanted. Her long and shiny jet black hair had been braided and the braids coiled up on each side of a perfectly shaped head above her little ears, pinned there by a flower broach. Her black almond eyes made my heart melt each time she fleetingly fixed her gaze on me. Her mouth was generous and her full and perfect lips parted as she spoke, showing a darting red tongue between snow-white and even teeth. Her small nose set off an altogether beautiful and attractive girl.

She would have been about 4ft 6ins, very petite, and she carried herself graciously erect. Her arms, waist and ankles were amazingly slender, yet she seemed quite energetic and sure of herself. Owing to the pyjama trousers and the loose top apparel of a bright flower print worn by the local younger women, it was hard to make out the lower body and leg outline. But her wisp of a waist curved out to show well rounded hips and a taut shapely bottom and I was, in a word, quite smitten by her.

Not least among her charms, in my eyes, was the shape of small breasts protruding under her top garment. This was unusual and itself made her unique and particularly attractive as the other girls had flat torsos. As we found out later to our disgust, it was still the custom, at least in rural areas, for females to bind their upper torsos until they had children at breast. This young girl had apparently escaped this queer practice.

After I had been asked several times which girl I fancied, I at last plucked up courage, as I realised the young one was not part of the entourage. Pointing to the daughter and addressing the madam, I said I only would go with this girl. All went quiet at this and the girl was asked to explain my request. On hearing the girl's hesitant interpretation, all the proceedings were upset and there was an uproar. I was told that the daughter was not selling her favours for any price and that the others were much better.

So, in company of another fellow who had also rejected the offers made to us, I returned very frustrated to the ship, where we were ridiculed for being such fussy fools and told of the wonderful exploits of the contented ones with their chosen partners. But I knew from the long and deep look I had received from the girl on leaving that I had pleased her very much with my choice. I also knew that I would see her again, for she was to me the star of the port and indeed of all Malaya. And I had money left, while the other lads had been about cleaned out.

I stayed aboard for a couple of nights. I was not ready to make the trip to the 'house of delight' by myself and try for her again. Then one day a shipmate and I took the dinghy and sculled over to an American ship to see what we could bum. After the usual explanation about life on a sailing ship, we told them about the port and were immediately asked if we knew where they could find a brothel.

We became instant entrepreneurs and offered to convey them out to our 'house' then back to their ship again for the fee of a girl for each of us. This was promptly agreed to and off we went ashore with a dinghy full of eager participants. There was great flurry at the house, girls were sent for and all were happy at this unexpected business turning up without the help of the 'pimp' son.

But even though I was number one boy on that day, my request for the girl was again promptly refused and I again returned aboard frustrated.

Her brother however had quietly suggested to me before I left that if I delivered another boatload of clients to the house, I could possibly buy his sister out for the evening, for a fee to him, as long as he came too as a chaperone.

This came about the next night and the girl readily agreed to the proposition, giving her mother assurances that nothing unbecoming would happen. We just wandered around the port with the brother in tow, having cool drinks and fruit. So it was again rather frustrating for me, even if, after a while of walking, she allowed me to hold her hand when we sat down on a park seat.

The girl, I will call her Ting Sui, as this is close to how her name sounded to my English ear, became quite talkative. She told me that her brother had been to high-school and was soon, at 18, to become the head of the family and go into business in Klang with a partner. Her father had been taken by the Japanese for forced labour during the occupation and had never returned. Her mother ran the brothel and was the breadwinner. This had allowed her brother and herself to be educated. For she was also attending high-school and both spoke better English than myself. Both also spoke Mandarin as well as their own Chinese dialect. Soon it was time for her to return home and for me to be back aboard again to dream of my new love.

Our next outing together, after I had deposited another boatload of hungry clients to their house, took place under the same awful conditions. But I asked Ting Sui if she liked me enough to want to be alone with me. On her consent, I put it to her brother that he should disappear. After a lot of haggling in their dialect he made a proposal to me: if I gave him a sum of money as 'insurance' for his sister's chastity and safe conduct (in fact a bribe) and if we swore to be back to meet him at an agreed time and never tell anyone, we could go off on our own.

All of this palaver was a lot for me to put up with but there was no other way to obtain what I wanted. The sum requested was quite considerable, but within my reach as I had, because of my obsession, saved quite a bit of money instead of spending my pay as my mates did on 'short-time' fees. On the next occasion, then, I handed over the bribe and at last Ting Sui and I went off together. She led me away from the village, slipping past her house and hamlet, along a path into the jungle.

After a short walk we stopped and waited to see if we were being followed, then we turned off the path, went through thick foliage, and came to an old tumbled down house with half its roof off. Inside we were at last alone in secret, under moonlight streaming through the empty windows and the rafters. We held each other and kissed longingly, which led next to exploring her trembling body.

At this point, and as I was allowed to unbutton her top, we were startled by a loud shriek. This temporally put us right off, and I scouted around to find the culprit. It was, we presumed, a monkey, and soon everything was quiet again. The interruption had allowed me to come to my senses and plan our next move. I found a dry half of a room and cleared all debris from this piece of planked floor. I then gathered a couch of soft ferns on which we could lay comfortably embraced.

Our passion was quickly rekindled, after disrobing, to boiling point. I lay caressing her small, lithe and trembling body. In the moonlight, against my tanned body, hers resembled ivory or marble. I kissed her eager mouth, our tongues entwining, exploring and tasting, I kissed her neck, gently biting her. Then to her sighs of delight I was kissing her hard little breasts. Oh how she tasted! Her body's fragrance was deliriously arousing. I methodically kissed her down to her belly button and then crouching and urging apart her already opening legs, gazed in wonder at the gorgeous girl. In the half light she seemed hairless on her mound, only on kissing her there could I discern soft hair like down.

Without more ado and with a panted 'Yes' for encouragement from Ting Sui I proceeded to kiss her deeply there and to excite her orally. She rose to my efforts, moaning with little sighs and gulps for breath.

At that age I was not very knowledgeable about women's physiology and their erotic responses. In retrospect, I am sure she reached climax, as all of a sudden she arched her back and grabbing my hair and ears whilst making awful and loud whimpering moans she squashed my face into her shaking and lunging body.

At last she released me and after regaining my breath I thought I was supposed to move fast. Whetting my middle finger I slid it into her to the hilt. At this she gasped, but this time not from passion. To my surprise I saw in her eyes only fear and hurt at me taking her virginity. On seeing some blood on my withdrawn finger she burst into tears. I was subdued for a while and lay cuddling her while telling her how much I wanted and loved her.

Soon I felt she had forgiven my unexpected intrusion and we were again engaged in passionate caresses. I presumed, as I had got this far again, that she would now be ready to go all the way, so kneeling between her open thighs I started to insert myself into her. At this she cried out and with a flick of her legs she was out from under me and had scrambled to her feet. I pleaded with her to let me have her, that she would enjoy it, that I would marry her. All entreaties were to no avail and all she would in the end do was, under my instructions, to satisfy me by hand. By this time we had to hurry back to the meeting place and her brother. I said goodnight to her after swearing I would never divulge to anyone what had happened between us. This love session had been enthralling in many ways, but eventually only half satisfying for me and apparently distressing for her. I returned on board relieved physically and still with the desire for more of her love and delights, but worried that she would not go out with me again because of my rude action of taking her virginity without her permission.

Despite my fear of having alienated Ting Sui's affection, my passionate encounters with her continued for a while. Of course our meetings depended on my ability not to be night watchman and to obtain the personal use of our pram dinghy, and also on the presence in port of ships with English-speaking crews interested in taking advantage of my offer to transport them to 'ultimate pleasure' at a very small cost.

*

Our cargo of sleepers was being steadily discharged into lighters and the hull was coming further up out of the water each day. As it did, the evidence of a foul bottom was there for all to see on the boot topping. Heavy cakes of barnacles and a lush crop of long weed were growing on the rusty scale of our hull. This would severely impair our passage through the sea on our future voyage. As it would be some time before the vessel could be dry-docked again for a complete 'hair-cut and shave', some partial clean-up was in order.

A few of us not on cargo or launch work were therefore detailed off to go over either side on a painting stage and remove this growth with scrapers. We then had to scale off the rust with scrapers and chipping hammers, after which as we worked down each fleet, and before shifting to the next fleet, we covered the bare metal with red lead. We stopped this work when the vessel reached her maximum permissible elevation and had to take in ballast to avoid the risk of becoming top heavy and turning over. The last few feet, from the stage drop down to the waterline, were taken care of by working from our dinghy.

To allow the maximum lift out of the water without losing stability, we sent down the three royal yards thus reducing the weight on the high tophamper.

For this delicate operation a heavy gantline was fed through a large metal block slung from a wire strop, rigged and shackled around the mast pole well above the yard. Buntlines and braces were unshackled and tied off, and a trip line was made fast to the yardarm on the side it was to descend on and led down to deck.

Weight was put on the gantline which was made fast an inch or two from the centre of the yard, and when the yard was lifted enough the parrel* traveller was unbolted from the truss. The yard's halyard and lifts were unfastened and tied off to the mast ready for when the yards were again crossed. Once freed from the lifts the yard 'cockbilled' to the vertical position owing to the gantline being affixed off centre. The gantline was gradually slacked away from the nearest deck capstan and the yard lowered to the deck, its descent guided clear of all rigging by the trip line. Once down, the three yards were securely lashed on deck.

The work over the side, although boring, occasionally had exciting moments. On one occasion Martin and I had rigged our stage, over the starboard side naturally, and scraped down and red-leaded the fleet to the last drop above the waterline. The stage was only a foot off the water in which our feet were submerged as we sat on it to complete the work down to the waterline.

The tide was on the ebb and the river current was running fast, carrying down lots of undergrowth ripped away from the banks up river by recent heavy rain. Martin was at one end of the stage and I was painting about the middle.

One second Martin was there, the next he was up the stage line and had launched himself over the gunwale and inboard where he reappeared pointing and shouting for me to come up off the stage. I looked to where he was pointing at his end of the stage and momentarily froze.

Sliding around the stage horns and the stage rope, the end of which was floating taut downstream in the current, was the moving body of a huge constrictor snake, glad to have found refuge and an escape from its journey out to sea. This boa or python had also been washed down the river and had grabbed the stage line as it floated by. We never saw its full length but its girth seemed as large as a dinner plate.

I was for a moment transfixed as it coiled itself out of the water, its head starting along the stage towards me. At the sudden thought of this monster enveloping and crushing me in its struggle to survive, I moved also like lightning. Throwing the paintbrush I had in my hand at the approaching reptile, I scrambled to my feet and was in two bounds along the stage up the rope and alongside Martin on deck.

The outcome of this interruption of work, noticed by the second mate, was to let go the lizards* and drop the stage in and out of the stream until, after several duckings, the snake gave up and abandoned its no longer dry and safe new haven. The mate was not amused at the loss of the paint brush and I got a berating for using a valuable tool as a missile in the confrontation.

As soon as we had finished our side and the other watch theirs, from stem to stern, we went over the whole area again by stage and dinghy, covering the red lead with green boot-topping paint, and below this we painted the couple of feet of the bottom that were now exposed with anti-fouling paint. This task completed, discharge of cargo was interrupted for a few days while we loaded and stowed two barges of mixed sand and stone ballast.

This unfortunately was to be our work this time as labour cost a lot more here than in South Africa. Stowing this ballast was backbreaking and the thought that we were going to have to dig it out at the other end, a much longer and still harder exercise, was thoroughly depressing. For the next two days it was a twelve-hour work day. At the end of each I was too exhausted to contemplate going ashore even on a promise.

We young lads seldom got a break from the shovel at driving a winch or handling the yard runner. We shovelled non-stop, trimming the continuous heap dumped from the never-ending queue of baskets coming inboard and down the hatch. We had to distribute ballast from side to side to a depth of 6 to 10 feet over a square area emptied of sleepers. As the height of ballast rose a brow or artificial bulkhead of heavy wooden limbers was built up at both ends of the ballast square to hold it in place.

When the 1,200 tons of ballast were in place in the three squares set out for the best stability, they were covered with boards to be chained down later when we departed port. As the ballast came in, heavy longitudinal shifting boards were also dropped in place to prevent any transversal movement if the ship lay over to any marked degree in heavy weather.

*

Ballasting completed, we went back to our routine while cargo discharge continued. I resumed my trips ashore, again taking 'clients' in the dinghy a couple of times, and I was able to carry on my steamy affair with Ting Sui, but achieved no further progress in my conquest.

Then, one Sunday when I was staying on board for a lazy day, as there were no new ships worth visiting, who should come up the accommodation ladder out of a sampan but Ting Sui herself! I had to look twice to realise it was her, as she had her hair down in braids and was in a frock.

She had found out how to visit the ship and paid the fare out to see me, with an excuse to her mother of visiting school friends. In this ruse she had enlisted the services of her brother as chaperone, so I was up for the usual fee to him when she left to go back ashore later that day by the boat that brought her out.

Most of my mates were off ashore for the day and I had a hard time borrowing to make up the sum. I showed her over the vessel and into our forecastle. I showed her where I slept, but I had no thought of using my bunk with her.

A few of the lads had brought girls back on board on occasions when they were lucky and had indulged in lovemaking behind their bunk curtains. Although most were as discrete as possible, all of us could hear what was taking place. I could not contemplate doing the same even though there was no one in the forecastle for a while. Anyone could come in at any time, and the idea of making love semi-publicly, so to say, did not appeal to me at all, as much as I desired Ting Sui.

But there was a solution, for I remembered our use of the sail locker for temporary quarters during the hurricane. So when the coast was clear we slipped into the locker, which was actually a lot larger than our forecastle, and I locked the door from inside. We climbed over the stow of sails to a comfortable spot lit by a nearby skylight. The rest was in darkness. It was dead quiet and pretty warm in there, which made a happy incentive to take our clothes off.

All this was exciting and fun for both of us, especially as I assured her that if by remote chance someone came to the locker, he would have to go for the key and we would have time to dress. We soon engaged in our usual formula of foreplay and this time I was enthralled to be rewarded by her telling me that, if I promised to be careful and to pull out early, then I could enter her.

Of course I promised and she guided me into her, telling me to be very gentle. I reassured her and I carefully forged deeply into her with, at first, regulated thrusts. Alas all went wrong again and I ruined a promising encounter once more. With the tight grip she exerted on me, causing a most unbelievable sensation, after only a dozen or so strokes that she started to enjoy, I lost all staying power, and with uncontrollable thrusts I climaxed into her prematurely, all thoughts of withdrawing having been abandoned.

On realising the situation she immediately cooled down. Crying for me to withdraw she angrily told me off for breaking my promise and pummelled me with her little fists. I had to quietly go for a bucket of water and a towel so she could wash herself.

Before her sampan picked her up at the gangway I had calmed her down, telling her of my undying love and promising to come back soon to marry her. I was not fooling at such promises. In my youthful naivety, I fully intended to keep my word, for I was very much in love with her. We made up and forgiving me she agreed to continue our relationship.

We met on two more occasions with no further upsets engineered by me. Then through a last shameful action of mine, the romance ended abruptly and sordidly.

A British ship came in, and as usual I accompanied a few of the crew ashore for a trip around to the 'house'. However they wanted to see Klang first. I knew I should have stayed behind, but thinking that if I did not stick with them they might not return to go around to the brothel (and therefore neither could I), I reluctantly went on the bus with them.

We visited a few shops, having a beer or two in most of them, and ended up in one where, after more bottles were consumed, we found ourselves in the company of young ladies. Soon the lads were for staying where they were and partaking of the wonderful selection of beauties at hand. I had noticed one and recognising this interest she quickly came over and sat on my lap. I said I did not want a girl but after more drinks and the offer of money to pay for the girl, my devotion to Ting Sui eventually evaporated in lust at the seductive enticement, kisses and fondling of this enchantress.

I capitulated to her power and we were soon in a room somewhere, copulating madly on a grass matt in the flickering light of an oil lamp. I never knew her name only that she was an Indian lass from Madras as she told me. I had noticed she was a Hindu, having the red paint spot on her forehead. She was brown-skinned with a lithe, slim but well-proportioned body.

She was very competent and agile in her attempt to fulfil me and tried various positions, until I was satiated owing to the combined effect of the beer and my half-conscious guilt.

With our plans thus upset, none of us wanted to go anywhere else when we got back to the port, and we returned to our ships. This ship sailed the following day and no other worth going aboard came in over the next few days. This turned out to be a godsend, especially for Ting Sui as I will explain.

After three days I had developed a stinging sensation in my penis which was painful when I passed water, and soon I had a yellowish discharge from there. I realised that I had caught VD, but wasn't sure what type. On asking the older men, I was told with some amusement that I had a dose of gonorrhoea.

I reported this to the captain who sent me ashore with the agent and I made a trip back up to Klang, this time to the hospital. I attended there on three occasions over the next week, twice receiving penicillin injections, and the last time a blood test.

Fortunately these visits took place in the morning and I did not bump into the brother at the jetty. I was eventually declared 'clean' again and thanked my lucky stars that we had not put to sea before I realised my ailment, or that I had not had the chance to meet again with Ting Sui since my escapade in Klang. If I had done so I would undoubtedly have passed on my ill-gotten disease to that innocent and trusting girl.

As it was, I was so ashamed of my actions and their consequences that I decided I could not face Ting Sui and so I stayed aboard till nearly sailing day.

On our final payday I slipped ashore and went to say goodbye to my Chinese friends at the shop. I had the feeling that my shameful behaviour and its apt punishment were known to them. I toyed with the challenge of going to say goodbye to Ting Sui, wondering how I would be received if she had caught wind of my infidelity. I was soon to find out.

As I walked down the main road I was of a sudden struck a stunning blow on the back of my head. Turning around to confront my assailant, I saw Ting Sui, who had now turned into a tigress, and was about to strike me again with the heel of a wooden soled slipper she was wearing. It was no good trying to remonstrate with her, as she was cursing me both in Chinese and in English, while continuing to belabour me. A circle of locals soon gathered to watch the scene and hear her accusations against this European who had wronged her.

The only thing to do was to turn and quickly walk away down the road to the jetty, to get any available boat to take me, ignobly, back to the ship, and to try to get over the shame of this public exposure of my guilt.

Ting Sui had evidently been told of my escapade in Klang and of my trips to the hospital. Not much could happen in a small port without becoming public knowledge. I realised the predicament Ting Sui had been put in by me. She had deceived her mother and to an extent her brother, even if he shared some blame for taking money to aid our affair. She would be able to cover the loss of her virginity as no one but us knew of our intimacy, but she would still feel the shame of having been spoiled and she would also lose face publicly for having been two-timed by a known 'suitor'. She had every right to consider that she had been used badly, and to hate me.

That was the sad and sudden end of my beautiful love affair. It was painful for me. I would have wanted to explain and ask for forgiveness but there was no time for this now and I knew it was best to leave things as they stood. I have often wondered what became of this lovely, trusting girl who once gave me her love and her virginity.

*

Christmas was upon us before the discharge was completed, our second Christmas aboard. It was a very ordinary one for us, a day off work and a few delicacies on the menu. Neither the Malays nor the Chinese celebrated Christmas so there was nothing different in the port. New Year, although not a special day for the locals either, was more interesting as it was celebrated by the administration.

It was made more memorable that year by the arrival of the British destroyer *Amethyst*. Most of her crew were given shore leave on New Year's eve. The usual incidents caused by rollicking sailors on such holidays developed into riotous behaviour particularly directed against the local Chinese, with stalls overturned and a few shops wrecked.

The reason for this hostility against the Chinese was that the British government, at this time of the civil war in China, had tried to use big-nation gunboat intimidation on the Chinese Liberation Army and had sent the *Amethyst* up the Yangtze river to shell the Reds. The Reds had retaliated and badly damaged the destroyer and of course Britain's prestige. Quite a few casualties were sustained including some killed. Now the warship and her crew were heroes in the UK and they were showing the colours on their way home after damage repairs in Singapore.

There were some more casualties and sore heads on New Year's day after the Navy pickets (police) had restored order and discipline of their men on shore. Those of us ashore that night kept well clear of these 'celebrations' and had no fraternisation with the Navy.

A few days later the last sling of our 60,000 sleepers came up out of the hold and went out over the side into the lighter, and we were all but ready for sea once more, ready at last to say farewell to the tropical paradise that had been our abode for nigh the past two months.

Chapter 7

BOUND FOR SOUTH AUSTRALIA

The 13th of January dawned quietly over our anchorage and the Malacca Strait. It was to be a long day for us, and a hot one. We turned out at 6am after a thirty-minute call and coffee made by the night watchman. We were soon sweating even though the sun had only just climbed above the horizon giving light to the humid jungle and the port inshore. Our donkey engine, primed and set to life at 5am, had engaged itself to its heroic task of shortening up the anchor, with a prayer from all of us that it did not falter. Several shackles of cable had been taken in the day before and so at 7.30 when the tug arrived we were about 'straight up and down' on the cable.

We were very pleased to see the tug pass up its own tow line to us: we would be spared the heavy job of pulling in our line when the tug cast off. Soon the anchor was away, free from the bottom and losing contact with the Malay Peninsula. As there was only a faint breeze the tug had to pull our dead weight for over twelve miles. Slowly, it towed us out past fishing villages on the islands off the port till we were in deep waters with room enough to set sail and to hold a course NE up the strait.

We worked through the day squaring up the vessel for sailing, coiling every line in its place, overhauling buntlines and testing all the gear. We picked up our watch at 1900 hours. It was a star-studded night and we slipped through the sea leaning over slightly under full sail and a favourable light breeze, making about 2–3 knots.

During my spell on lookout I fell in deep thoughts over our recent oriental interlude. I was devastated at the way my all-important romance had ended and to a certain extent was wallowing in self-pity.

Being ashamed of my actions and utterly furious at myself, I had expressed these sentiments to my shipmates. Their response was rather predictable. Not to worry about it. Plenty more fish in the sea. Sailors fall in love in every port. Put it down to experience. Girls must expect such conduct, etc. One interesting fact I was given, I suppose to alleviate my guilt, was the ease with which a woman can hide her prior loss of maidenhood and fool her husband on the wedding night.

Given that a woman's virginity was for centuries an essential requirement of a marriage (and still is in many countries today, as it was of course in Malaya amongst all its ethnic communities at the time) women have everywhere devised ingenious ways of fooling their partners. It was apparently an age-old practice to insert at the crucial time before the act a pellet of dried chicken blood. It melted during intercourse and the husband, espying blood at withdrawal, was convinced of his bride's full value and virtue as well as of his own male valour.

What was implied, of course, when I was told this story, was that I did not have to worry about Ting Sui's future. However nothing said could alter the feeling I had of having done wrong and my impression that my bout of VD (the only such casualty among our crew) looked very much like divine punishment for my being unfaithful.

The stern dismissal I had received from my 'little Asian flower' also brought back memories of Pamela. I had not thought of her for a long time, and in fact I realised that I now had only a gone feeling for her. Although I have always fondly remembered her, she already belonged to another world. I no longer felt any resentment for her quickly aborted attempt at maintaining a relationship with me, understanding in the light of the recent events that she had made the right decision. What a poor future she would have had with a seafarer who would have been absent most of her life and who could not control his roving amorous impulses!

These two love affairs, however, left me with a certain sense of emptiness at this time. So did of course the thought of no longer having a home to go back to, after my mother's 'desertion'. Not that I bore Mum any grudge for this entirely justified action. I had had time to come to terms with these events since I received the news in South Africa. But I regretted to be so far away from her in the circumstances.

I was not homesick but was worried about her present welfare. Letters were few and far between as sea mail was slow. If we had already sailed when any mail arrived at a port, then it was sent on to our next port of call, sometimes missing us again. This worry kept nagging me throughout our voyages, especially in moments of rest, when I was alone, for instance on lookout duties in calm weather as I was on that first night of our passage to Spencer Gulf.

*

All these deep thoughts were suddenly shattered when a fast freighter, that I should have spotted and reported, overhauled us in no time at all and illuminated us with a searchlight as it passed. It was an American, the *Steel Fabricator*. It hailed us over its loud speaker, wishing us 'bon voyage' and gave us three blasts on its siren. Owing to the surprise and excitement of this sudden incident no one remembered to admonish me for not reporting the vessel coming up astern, but it was indeed serious negligence on my part as we could well have been run down in such a situation with only a dull stern light showing.

Collisions between steamships and sailing vessels were a common occurrence in earlier times when a fair percentage of the world's tonnage was still sail-driven. Then it was very often the steamship that was run down. The latter had nearly always misjudged the speed of a sailing vessel downwind and presumed they could safely cut across her bows instead of altering course and diverting astern.

Our ship, when a Flying P liner under the German flag, had two collisions under such circumstances within twelve months of each other. The first time she sank the Frenchman *Daphne* that had tried to cross her bows in clear daylight not realising how fast the *Passat* was going down the English Channel. On her next voyage out of Hamburg to Chile she cut down a British steamship, again in the Channel. On neither case was the *Passat* at fault. Both times she suffered some damage about the bowsprit, but her stem, which was like a sharpened ram, dealt a fatal blow to the offender.

We must have been a grand sight in the beam of the *Steel Fabricator*'s searchlight. But not as fine as we would have if we had been fully loaded. No vessel appears at her best high out of the water when 'light ship'.

Soon after this episode dark clouds covered the sky, blackening out the stars and leaving the night like ink. We wore ship at midnight in a rain squall, and went on the other tack. So passed an eventful sailing day and we were very glad to climb into our bunks.

The voyage down to South Australia's Spencer Gulf proved a slow one. It took a week to beat up the strait and round the north of Sumatra. We were forced to wear and tack ship continually. Rain squalls, electric storms generating every type of lightning, were in abundance, often cutting visibility even in daylight to only a few feet, so that when peering forward from the foredeck the jib-boom would disappear out of sight. In such circumstances our hand-cranked foghorn had to be put to use.

I can still hear its monotonous, mournful howl. The infernal machine was sounded by the lookout for a full minute at three-minute intervals. Lookouts always had to be posted at any time visibility was reduced to the point of making normal navigation unsafe. This was even more necessary with us owing to our lack of manoeuvrability.

Between squalls we often had blue skies and a clear horizon, though never enough wind to blow it all away. When these breaks occurred, all could see the need for sounding a warning of our presence, as often we were surrounded by small craft, many quite close. Junks were the majority. Some were under sail power, with lantern sails hoisted on three masts on the larger ones, while others were motorised.

One motorised craft made a full circle around us, and we suspected it could have been a pirate. If it was it gave us a miss, possibly realising that we had no cargo and that whatever else of value we might carry would certainly not warrant the effort of boarding us, which would have been an easy exercise for them.

A Standard Oil tanker, the *Stanvac Sydney*, altered course and came over to inspect us. We also sighted a P & O passenger liner coming down the strait probably headed for Penang. However she did not divert to look us over. She could have been late on her schedule, or maybe mistook us for a mirage.

On rounding again the north tip of Sumatra we were prevented from making a good course south by a combination of headwinds and the current from the NE monsoon. So for another two weeks we made a lot of westing with leeway. By the time we passed the latitude of the Cocos Islands we were in a longitude nearly due south of Ceylon. We were approximately 18° S and 85° W before we caught the real force of the SE trade winds. These proved to be very strong in the Indian Ocean and we were soon making headway, at least in a SSE direction, going from one tack to another, braced hard up either way.

The chief mate, on this voyage, had become even more obsessed with preservation of his sails. Consequently our watch would set all the canvas necessary, within safety limits, to obtain the maximum speed from the wind blowing at the time. Then the mate's watch came on deck under the third mate, but as soon as the mate himself appeared he would order a reduction in the sails set. Or at night, before he went below and left the watch to his junior, he would shorten down with orders not to set any more sail. This charade went on watch after watch. In came upper topgallants, crossjack, and flying jib and gaffs, often even the main course, then out we would set them again.

Our day work for a while at this time was a dirty one. It consisted of first tarring down shrouds and other rigging, then white-leading the fore and back stays. The technique we used for this job was to rig a gantline on a lizard or block at the head of each stay. Sometimes a single position at the head of a set of stays would do to service three stays.

On the top end of the gantline a boatswain's chair was made fast by the seaman who was to ride and work in it, with a double sheet bend. Above the bend you then coupled together the gantline and the stay along which you were to come down, with a harp shackle. You climbed into your chair after affixing a bucket of mixed white lead and tallow to one side. Then, with one hand, you pinched the two parts of the gantline together so as to hold yourself suspended temporarily in this position.

With the other hand you hauled up some slack, which you held with your teeth while you took another reach, till enough slack was drawn up to pass the bight over your head, down your back, under the chair and your feet, then up again to form a hitch back on itself when the slack went through and it tightened just under the sheet bend. Now you were ready to slack away on your gantline with one hand while with the other you applied the whiting using a rag soaked in the bucket.

A quicker way of lowering was also used: it was to affix a heavy meat hook to the standing part of the gantline, a little way above the chair, then instead of making the former hitch with the hauling part, you passed this part as before through the apex of the chair's legs but then up and over the hook where it hung straight up and down. The weight of this part of the line, leading down to the deck into a coil there, just about held you in position. That was until you had descended further down and this weight balance no longer operated fully. You then had to control your lowering by stoppering the hauling part between your knees and feet or more deftly, if you were barefoot, by using your toes. This latter method could be dangerous and needed constant attention; otherwise you could descend at an accelerating pace and splatter your body over the deck below. It was a choice of adjusting safety with speed and skill.

Many jobs required the use of both arms and hands, and even teeth, when up aloft, especially when furling sail in a fair strength of wind. So it was absolutely necessary to use your feet and in many cases a knee grip in order to have both arms free while dangling at any height aloft. The motto of 'one hand for yourself and one for the ship' is irrelevant on sailing ships. If any crew member applied it, other than occasionally to steady himself against falling, he would render himself useless and the crew would be a man short on the job.

All this may sound like risky acrobatics to the reader, but all work aloft is actually accomplished with a fair margin of security. Despite appearances, seamen are mostly far from reckless. Indeed they frown upon anyone performing unnecessary stunts likely to put the whole crew at risk or to generate extra work. I can illustrate this point with an incident where I was myself guilty of stupid overconfidence and indulged in a display of bravado that could have ended with my demise. I escaped harm, but my behaviour made me lose some hard-won points of respectability among the crew, at least for the rest of the run to the Gulf.

We were on watch one day whilst drifting with no wind in the Indian Ocean on the edge of the SE trades. The second mate noticed that a buntline shackle pin had come adrift and that the shackle had come out of the splice at the end of the buntline wire, thus allowing the wire to part from the foot of the upper topgallant sail on the main mast, and slip upwards out of the fairlead guides on the forepart of the sail. The wire had been finally stopped when the splice jammed itself in the starboard outer buntline block affixed to the jackstay on that yard. The second mate blew two whistles to summon the watch to brail up the sail so that the buntline could be re-rove and shackled back onto the foot of the sail by a man going aloft, after which the sail could be reset.

Seeing there was no wind and the sail was hanging up and down, I declared with cocky assurance that I could fix the problem myself without the watch having to take in the sail. I explained my plan and was told to go ahead. All went well at first. Up I went with a spare shackle hanging by rope yarn around my neck, out along the yardarm to the buntline block concerned. I overhauled the buntline so I had excess slack to work with. I then slid a gasket along the jackstay until it was alongside the block, I undid the gasket, put a bowline* in the bottom to stand in, then let this fall over the fore part of the sail. There it hung perfectly and I could even glimpse the lower topgallant yard I would exit onto from the gasket when finished.

Over I went down the gasket, reeving the buntline through its fairleads as I went. Sitting in the bowline I shackled back the buntline splice to the foot of the sail. Just as I was about to reach out with a toe to pull myself in to the yard and transfer to it, a wind appeared from nowhere filling our sails. My particular sail was bellied out hard and now positioned me way out from my means of exit, and dangling over space. I tried to climb back up, but with the weight of myself and the wind pressure on the canvas under the gasket, now contoured to the belly of the sail, I could not slip my hand under the gasket and get a grip so as to climb.

I was marooned here in this precarious position, so it seemed, for as long as the wind persisted, which could have been for days. My mind was set: I was not going to call for help even in the face of death. Trying to climb up the sail again and again, only to be defeated time after time, I eventually tired and became desperate. At this point I decided to use my feet to prise a space between the gasket and the canvas so as to get a further grip to climb. This proved successful for a few grips upwards, but tiring fast I started to panic at realising that I would not make it to the top and the yard, and that I had only two alternatives left: either slide back down to the bowline and wait to be ignobly rescued in the end if the wind did not desist, or, ultimate punishment of my stupidity, let go and fall to eternity.

With these alternatives in mind I made a final move to extricate myself and kicked out with what strength I had left. I felt the canvas give way at the seam on the point of impact. I was past giving any thought to the damage I was doing and the retribution I would sustain. I soon kicked a hole in the sail big enough for me to pass through, swung myself through this rent panel and slid down to the yard below which was now within reach. On reaching safety at last I could not help thinking of what would have happened had the sail been brand new and not an old fair-weather one. I could not have accomplished such a smart escape, unless I had used my knife and then suffered the dire consequences of such a sacrilege!

I descended to the deck in shame to be castigated by all. Not only did the watch now have to brail up the sail, they had to cut it adrift and send it down, put it in the sail locker, get another one out, send this one up and bend it on, and finally set it. An initial twenty-minute job was turned into a two-hour one all down to me. My retribution in the end for this folly was to spend the next three afternoon free watches repairing the ruined sail cloths. I was very relieved to be let off so lightly, as the cost of new canvas involved in my repair could have been deducted from my pittance of a wage.

This episode was a lesson for me and I had to eat humble pie for a while till I won back the respect I had gained the hard way since I joined. Fortunately the new hands did not seem to take any notice of my fall from grace. It was possibly my own worry at what others were thinking of me and my unrealistic sense of self-importance that was being challenged as I matured.

This second year had certainly seen a difference in the application of discipline. From the initial system of 'make or break you', with cuffs and kicks meted out to one by any in rank above if one did not comprehend quickly enough or dared to step out of line, it had toned down to mostly verbal discipline, with only an occasional blow for a good reason from a mate. The pecking-order rules were relaxed somewhat as well, even allowing the food kit to be passed round to any who asked, instead of ABs then OSs having first and second pick and boys contending for what was left.

However I recognise there was good reason for the draconian and somewhat cruel discipline, by today's standards, which we experienced during the first six months. It was the only way, taking additional language problems into consideration, whereby such a green crew, the majority of whom were first-trippers, could be moulded into an efficient, willing and organised workforce. Those in command were responsible for the ship's safety, and indeed for our own lives, and they had to ensure that we were fit and capable enough to even begin, let alone complete, such a hazardous voyage.

*

When our jobs aloft were completed and when all the tar and lead were removed from the wooden decks and the latter holystoned and scrubbed white, we started scraping and red-leading the bulwarks and bulkheads after soogying them down. Then we painted these areas first with undercoat, then with white topcoat. And when all was finished the inboard of our vessel looked just fine.

After 32 days trying to beat south so as to turn east with the westerlies, we at last picked them up in Lat. 38° S, Long. 85° E. We braced away on the starboard tack heading for a position well south of the south-west point of Australia. As the wind gained force our day run increased, although often well handicapped by our mate's continually ordering a reduction of sail for no reason in our opinion.

We were now far from the tropics and the weather had cooled, even though it was still summer in the southern hemisphere. Soon we were on the edge of the Roaring Forties and our day work, apart from the rigman's work, was restricted to splicing, touching up paint and bright work and any other useful jobs that could be dropped immediately if the watch was needed for sailing work. These small jobs could be performed only because we were light ship. If we had been fully loaded, the only job that could have been performed would have been making sennet* for chafing gear on the stays.

This chafing gear was made from rope yarns and, when needed, was wound round those parts of the rigging that came into constant contact with any of the sails when set. It prevented to a great extent the premature wearing out of canvas by chafing against wire rope stays, especially when the vessel was becalmed and the sails swung back and forth with our rolling in the swell. This menial task could be accomplished when the watch was standing by under the forecastle and the decks were continuously awash with seas. It was known as 'gainful occupation', a euphemism for a job to give the men when they cannot do anything else (for a crew should never be left idle in daytime!).

At times when running free, below the Great Australian Bight, we logged some very good speeds for the sail we had set at the time. Our trim was good and being, as I said, light ship, it was great to tear along in this manner with, at most times, dry decks.

About halfway across the longitude of the Bight we made a course north of east so as to come up to our entry to Spencer Gulf somewhere between Cape Spencer and Cape Catastrophe. Soon we sighted a few ships as we came up to the sea lane of general shipping, so lookouts were doubly vigilant to give early warning of anything in our path.

We now prepared and catted our anchors. On 1st March we sighted land at 1700 hours and then made out a further headland indicating that we were not far out from our expected landfall. I considered this another navigational feat, as our compass was well out and we had had little opportunity of regular positioning by sightings at noontimes.

By the end of our evening watch (7–12pm) we were passing Neptune Island and were into the Gulf. We wore ship in the morning at eight bells, and squared away for Port Victoria, halfway up the Yorke Peninsula on the far side of the Gulf. On this final lap we crossed by an Australian coaster the *Iron King* which passed close astern as we tacked ship at noon. At 9pm we were called out from our bunks, being watch below, and with the port watch started the long, hard, but this time pleasant task of shortening down our sail.

By 11pm on 2nd March 1948, with all furled but the last few sails to bring us up to our decided position, we dropped the starboard anchor approximately two miles off the Wauralteee light. After a rather long run, considering the actual port-to-port distance, of 49 days from Port Swettenham, we were once again attached to *terra firma* by our anchor's cable.

Chapter 8

SPENCER GULF

The First World War saw the end of the coal trade out of Newcastle, NSW, for sailing ships. This trade had employed the world's last regular sail carriers, mainly large steel four-mast barques, sailing from Europe with whatever they could corner of general cargo freight that steamships had passed over. At times they even made the long haul out to Australia in ballast.

They assembled at Newcastle to wait in queue for a cargo of coal for the west coast of South America. After discharging in one or two of the many ports down the Chilean and Peruvian coasts, they would backload a cargo of nitrate (chemical fertiliser) or guano (natural fertiliser of compounded bird droppings) and carry this to Europe. In the 1920s only Germany and France remained in this trade, now sailing out and back via Cape Horn.

But by the end of the 'twenties only Germany persisted, owing to the French government cancelling the subsidy that had kept French ships in this trade on an economical basis. The Germans hung on only thanks to their talent for organisation and their final effective monopoly of stevedoring operations which enabled their ships to be turned around in the shortest time. This advantage, in addition to their prowess at building and crewing large vessels strong enough to make two round voyages per year instead of one, allowed them to turn in a profit and never have to rely on a subsidy. It was on the presumption that the trade would continue after the war that the Laeisz company had built two more ships, the *Priwall* in 1919, and in 1926 the *Padua* which was the epitome of the commercial sailing vessel. They both made amazingly fast passages out and back to Europe via the Horn. However with the development of chemical fertilisers in Europe even this trade petered out by the later 'thirties. The last crack German sailers were diverted in the end to the grain trade.

The once prosperous timber trade from the west coast of North America had also finished by the 1920s. This left only the grain trade as the last bastion of commercial sail. The grain trade boom was due mainly to a growing demand for grain to feed the increasing population of Europe. This demand gave impetus to wheat growing in Australia, especially around Spencer Gulf where returned soldiers, after the First World War, took advantage of generous government loans to establish new farms. The opportunity was there for a regular trade, but it was viable only if this commodity could be transported at the cheapest possible expense. There was no finance available for the development of a modern infrastructure for the transport of the goods from the farms to the ports or for storage, nor were there any major ports around the Gulf with modern loading facilities at deep wharves. The grain trade was therefore only practical with the use of nineteenth-century methods of stevedoring and sailing ships, which offered the lowest freight costs and were ideally suited to these conditions. There was no pressure of time as long as a steady stream of grain shipments arrived in Europe the year round to top up the normal local supply.

This gave the last lease of life to the condemned few surviving from the former great fleets of sailing ships.

In the inter-war years as many as thirty of these ships would sail into the Gulf and disperse to several loading ports, Germein, Lincoln, Wallaroo and Victoria. Germein had no loading wharf. Because of this and the cost of wharfage increasing in Wallaroo and Lincoln for the building of silos and bulk loading infrastructure, Port Victoria became the main loading point and in fact it was the only one left after the Second World War when Port Germein closed down.

In 1949, with the last shipment of grain on a sailing vessel, Victoria also closed as a port. The *Passat* and *Pamir* after discharging in the UK were handed back to Germany and were later employed in the grain trade from Argentina to Hamburg till 1957.

*

Our final anchorage, after a shift on the next day with the agent and harbour master aboard, was still off Wauraltee Light and Wardang Island, approximately two miles out from the main jetty which ran out from the sea end of the township's main road.

Near to us at anchor was our old companion the *Viking*, and further along was the bald-headed four-mast barque *Lawhill*. The latter, who was under South African flag at that time, was half loaded and was to sail back to South Africa on a run she had made quite a few times during the war. As to the *Viking*, who was like us due for Europe, she had already started loading.

As we were the last to arrive we had low priority for service until the *Lawhill* was full and sailed. Our initial job was to ready the lower hold, apart from the ballast squares, to receive an initial tonnage of bags. This consisted in laying dunnage and separation cloth of burlap on the ceiling and up the sides of the hold after a final clean-out of bilges and an inspection by the consignees. Then, for several weeks, we only received cargo when the other two vessels' working arrangements released a small craft out to us.

Loading methods were primitive. To transport the bagged grain out to the deep-watermen anchored in the stream there were two schooners and two ketches. One of the schooners was a beautiful three-mast vessel with a long old-fashioned bowsprit over a jib-boom. After work had finished for the day these small sailers berthed overnight at a small wharf further around from the township.

The main jetty was the centre point for the loading operations. The grain was brought in by flat-top trucks from storage barns on the outskirts of the township or directly from the farms when the barns became empty during the loading season. The trucks brought the bags to the beginning of the jetty where they were restacked by hand onto a four-wheel rail flat-top. A horse hauled the flat-top down the rail line to the end of the jetty. There the bags were slid down a shoot by hand into the hold of one of the small vessels, where they were again stacked. When the small vessel was fully loaded it ran out to one of the deep-watermen and tied up alongside. Once in position by the hatch into which the bags were to be loaded, the ketch or schooner would stay there until its consignment was sent up over the side and down the hold of the deep-waterman. Depending on its capacity it could be alongside till dusk. So in all, each bag of grain was handled at least seven times from the shore stack to stowage in a vessel's hold.

The slings of bags, fourteen bags in each, were made up on the feeder vessel by the ketch's crew and maybe one or two locals. The last bags loaded onto the feeder were already laid into a sling so that they could be sent down the hold quickly as soon as the feeder was tied alongside, making room for the preparation of the next sling. In most cases there was never any waiting: when the hook arrived back over the side another sling of bags was ready to be hooked on.

The men that worked down below, the stowing gang, were at first local lumpers. Later, when the *Lawhill* had sailed and the *Viking* was nearing completion, we had the surplus lumpers from those jobs come out to us. These were mostly men from Port Adelaide who had come around for the season. They stayed in Port Victoria's only hotel or boarded with locals. They came out on the first feeder in the morning as did the locals and went ashore on the last feeder when she finished.

South Australian lumpers had a peculiar method of carrying bags. Whereas in most places it is customary to carry bags on the shoulder, here they were carried low down on the back resting in the hands. For me, who later used the common method, this would have restricted my ability to flick or toss the bags in exactly the place I wanted them to lay. However they seemed to have no difficulty in achieving the result they wanted.

The stowing method was to build first a stack or block of bags (10 x 10 x 6) on the ceiling (bottom) of the hold. Then two men worked on the top of the stack receiving the slings and dispensing the bags individually onto the backs of the 'runners'. These carried the bags out on each side to the wings of the hold and placed them one on another, six high, starting from the wing perimeter and moving in towards the stack. Gradually the space between the cargo battens on the ship's side and the stack would reduce, until the last line of bags was dropped from the stack into the hole left for them. This exercise would cover the hold space with layers of bags six high.

Then the whole process would be repeated, starting with another stack, until the hold was filled to the deckhead. The only departure to this method was when the area to be filled was not the full area of the hold, such as where the ballast square was. In this case a 'brow' was built by turning every other bag as in a corner of brickwork. This bound the edge in, so that when the ballast was taken out from its square the face, some thirty bags or more high, would not collapse and spew into the vacated area. So a certain amount of skill was necessary for the safe stowage of bagged grain.

The size of the lumper gangs was generally two on deck (one on the nok drum and one on the winch), and twelve below, that is, two on the stack, four runners on each side of the stack and two extras to spell the runners. Some runners wore a leather cap with a flap hanging down to protect their neck. Others wore a full back cover. Most worked barefoot as this gave better footgrip and balance when running over the layers of placed bags with a burden.

*

Port Victoria was the last outpost of bagged grain export using old methods of stevedoring. In 1947, although called a port, this small settlement was only a village on the coast which had grown around a jetty that serviced the shipment of the grain produced in that area of the Yorke Peninsula.

It was situated halfway down the west coast of the peninsula. The main road led from the jetty through the village for a third of a mile. This portion was surfaced. It then continued unsurfaced, through wheat paddocks for approximately twenty miles to a small town called Maitland. From there the road ran NNE and then turned east and joined up near Port Wakefield with the road coming down from Augusta and Pirie. So the road rounded the top of St Vincent's Gulf and then continued down its east coast to Adelaide, a distance of approximately 130 miles from Port Victoria.

The permanent population was only about 450 but grew in the loading season and also at holiday times when people from inland came to the coast. The whole area was flat and dry but had enough rainfall in normal years to produce rich harvests of wheat.

Near the jetty, at the beginning of the road, was situated the hotel. The village boasted a school, a church and a hall in which a picture show was run two nights a week, while we were there anyway. Up the road on either side were a general store, a newsagent cum post office, a bank, a butcher's shop, a milk bar and restaurant, and perhaps one or two other shops that I have forgotten.

The township had a one-man police station with lockup (this number was at times reinforced to two, three or four officers depending on how many deep-watermen were anchored off and the amount of labour staying in town to work them). At the end of the surfaced road was a garage which was also the depot for the buses. The bus company ran services to Maitland and Minlaton twice a day, and most days there was a bus leaving for Adelaide and one returning from there.

Further around the bay, past the small-craft jetty where our feeder boats tied up at night or when not employed, was a row of about sixteen holiday huts owned by people from the farms or from inland townships who used them for their seaside holidays each year.

Some of the huts were not securely locked. On several occasions when the weather was rough and we could not get back to our ship after a session at the hotel till 9pm, we secretly spent the night in one of them. We arranged a watch roster of an hour or so, the last one being in charge of waking us up in the morning. At times when we knew there would be no boat for us we would have a whip-round (what we called a 'tarpaulin muster') to raise enough to buy a flagon or two of cheap wine before we set off for the huts. We would make hot toddy by adding sugar and raisins to the rough wine and cooking this brew over a primus stove. Most of these huts had such items stored in them. We would tell yarns and sing songs till we were lulled into a deep sleep in comfortable and snug bunks. The huts were far enough from other habitation so we were never reported to or found by the local constabulary. We always left the huts as we found them.

Sometimes when stranded after the pictures we used the grain sheds, sleeping on the bags with a couple of empties for a blanket.

I generally only came ashore on pay night or after work on a Saturday for I was broke on all other occasions.

The pub was the meeting place for all the crews and the lumpers. For us lads, we suffered the same pecking order ashore as we did aboard. We never got into arguments. I was not a great drinker and could not have afforded to drink much even if I had been. There were a few incidents and fights, more within crews than between crews from different ships. Only on one occasion do I recollect the police being called. Two fellows from another ship were locked up for the weekend and then bailed, fined and discharged on the Monday morning. In most cases there was good comradeship between all, including the shore people.

The younger fellows would often gather at the milk bar and talk to the local lads. There were never any girls of our age there as these were kept at home after dark or chaperoned when they went out. The only girls around were the owner's daughters. The older one, who was about fifteen, served behind the counter and in the restaurant. There was no chance of even taking her to the pictures. Her little sister, a pretty blond of about ten years, therefore received most of the attention as she was allowed to mix with us. I am sure she thought she was a star celebrity being given several presents of Chinese origin that we had brought from Malaya. She even scored a model of the ship from one fellow.

On a couple of occasions we were invited to go 'spotlighting'. This was a night hunt for foxes and rabbits in trucks or pickups. We would drive into the scrub and paddocks then park, turning off the lights. Then with a strong spotlight we swept the area in search of rabbits. When caught in the beam, the rabbits were mesmerised and crouched still. We could see their eyes glowing and they were an easy target to shoot or even pick up by hand.

After two or three hours we would have up to a hundred rabbits strung up on the vehicle and would call a finish. Very few foxes were shot for they are very cunning. When hearing humans they go to ground. Anyway, it was foolish, in my opinion, to kill foxes as they helped to keep the rabbit population somewhat in control. Rabbits were classed as vermin there, and in fact all over Australia, for they multiplied enormously in a good season.

On one weekend I was invited by a local lad that I had palled up with to go to a Saturday night dance with some other youths. We left in the mid-afternoon in a truck and after picking up other lads around the area we drove up to the metropolis of Maitland, parked the vehicle and had a few beers at all the town's hotels.

At the last one we had a meal in the dining room before picking up our beverages for the evening from the bottle shop. Whilst having our meal I got talking to the lass who waited on our table and who turned out to be the hotel cook's daughter. She was also going to the dance with her friends after she finished her work on the tables and helped her mother strap up the kitchen, and she told me she would see me at the hall. This was encouraging but then I realised she would expect me to be able to dance, which I could not. However it was a start and the night was young.

Before going into the dance hall we hid our personal bottles of wine in the bushes of the garden. The hall was a large wooden structure about the size of a barn with a stage at the far end where the band performed. There were chairs down both sides. On one side sat and stood the females and on the other side stood and sat the males, some smoking, and all eyeing off their hoped-for dance partners on the other side.

The procedure for the whole evening was rather peculiar. When the band struck up a dance they could perform, the fellows hurried across the floor to ask the female they fancied for the dance. Sometimes one or two would be unlucky, being refused or beaten by others. These then looked for a second choice if any were left. If there were none or they were refused again, they returned to their side of the floor, frustrated and with their ego deflated somewhat. I did not have to run this risk as I could not dance a step. All I could do was watch the lass I had spoken to earlier being glided around by others and looking at me quizzically when passing by me.

At one time between the dances she beckoned me to follow her when she went out to the toilet at the back with her friend. I followed and was asked why

I had not invited her for a dance. She was disappointed when I told her that I longed to dance with her but was not a dancer.

However I said that I liked her and wanted to see her more, so would she come outside to see me after the next break since we could not converse inside. At the next break in the dancing quite a few from both sides went outside including my desiree and her friend. I followed with my local mate and we led them to a shady nook by our stashed grog for some refreshments.

The girls would not drink our cheap wine straight, so we all went to a milkbar for lemonade and nabbed a glass on the way out. We talked and the girls drank their mixed drinks from the glass. We wanted to cuddle up but they were not having that. Nevertheless they agreed to come out again to our spot next time. This continued till our liquor supply was exhausted.

By this time the dance was about over and we met them outside where all the fellows from Port Victoria agreed to meet back at the truck at 1am after walking our new partners home. I walked the lass, whose name was Barbara, back to the hotel where she lived. She took me through the yard and up a set of steps to the back verandah where there was a row of beds along the wall, all empty.

This was an ideal opportunity offered to my carnal instincts and we were soon cuddling and cavorting on one of the beds. Despite my determination not to squander such an opportunity, she offered prolonged token resistance and time ran away on us. When I had at last melted her resistance with pleas and foreplay it was way past my 1am deadline. So although at last satisfied I was then worried as to how I was to return to Port Victoria. She told me to stay and sleep where I was and explained that I could catch the bus in the morning. Then off she went to her quarters and to bed.

It was after 9am in the morning when the lass woke me to tell me I had missed the bus. Maybe she was taking revenge or maybe, I thought egotistically, she was entrapping me to stay in the town. She went away and came back with some cold breakfast as I finished washing myself. I explained to her that I had to return or the captain would have the police search for me and we would all be in trouble, but I promised I would see her again and in fact would come up again on the following weekend.

Somewhat spruced up I said farewell and snuck out through the yard down the street and onto the road to Victoria. I was confident of soon hitching a lift and was after a mile pleasantly comforted when an old car came along and stopped for me. The old fellow who drove it told me to jump in. Unfortunately he was turning off the road to his property only a few miles further but he said that I would soon get another lift.

But nothing else on wheels came along and I ended up walking all the way. The road was unsurfaced and dusty. By midday I was sweating, what for the heat of the day, what for the continuous exertion of fighting the swarms of flies. I would beat them off then try to outrun them for a hundred yards or so, but they would catch me up again invading my nostrils, my eyes and even my mouth if I opened it to curse my predicament. The distance seemed interminable compared with the run up in the truck.

At last I came over a slight rise, and there was Port Victoria and the *Passat* at anchor. My ordeal was not over though, for when I eventually reached the jetty our motorboat was on its way in. One of the mates coming ashore informed me, shaking his head, that the captain would expect to see me in the morning at 9am. At last after waiting till 9.30pm for our boat to return to the ship I stepped aboard tired, broke and hungry. Still, even with the worry of the impending meeting with the master on the morrow and the fear of the likely penalty, I turned in with the comfort that it had all been worth the trouble.

*

Several times I was invited by locals on a boat excursion to Wardang Island to harvest mutton birds or shearwaters. But I declined after hearing of how the birds were caught and killed. The 'harvest' consisted of pulling the baby chicks out of the burrows where they had been hatched and snapping their necks. I could never have done that or been a spectator to this ruthless massacre. I would have to be very hungry to resort to such a way of obtaining a feed. Thousands of these birds flock each year to nest on islands free of animal predators. Now human predators have invaded their islands and are taking their chicks. Mutton bird meat is not even very nice. I did try some and I found it very fishy and oily.

Another excursion I was able to make was to Adelaide, the capital of the state of South Australia. This came about unexpectedly when word came out to the ship that a relative of mine had arrived on the bus to see me. I got the rest of the day off from the mate and was able to take advantage of our motor launch ferrying the agent ashore.

The relative in question turned out to be a great uncle on my mother's side. In other words, my Australian grandmother's brother, Uncle George.

My grandfather, who was a carpenter in London, emigrated out to Australia as a young man in the 1890s to make his fortune. It was when working inland in the Queensland bush at a place called Goondiwindi that he had met and married my grandma, who had been born and bred in Queensland. After working around north and central Queensland as well as in Brisbane at his much sought-after trade, he had earned enough to return to England with his bride and eventually start a building firm in Wimbledon, south-west London.

During the First World War, when my mother was a girl, Uncle George fought in France with the Australian forces and he came over to London on leave a couple of times. Ever since, my mother had been a favourite of his and they had corresponded each Christmas.

I can remember first being told of him by my mother when a parcel of chocolate, dried fruits and other goodies arrived from Australia during the Second World War. This is how I learned that I was a quarter Australian.

So my mother had written to Uncle George and told him I was coming to Spencer Gulf. He was no longer living in Brisbane but stayed with his son and his family in Adelaide. He had found out from the Adelaide agents the port where the *Passat* was loading.

We talked about the family, and he asked if I could come to Adelaide for a few days, explaining that I would have to find digs there, as his son had no spare room at his place, but that he would pay for my accommodation. Uncle George was of course an old man to me, and a stern one at that, it seemed. But he offered to show me around and the fact that I would be staying on my own made the prospect attractive. I agreed to ask for leave and come up as soon as it was granted.

Once again the master, on the promise that I would give my address on arrival to the agent's main office in Port Adelaide, report there by telephone each day and be back for duty on the date he prescribed, accepted to let me go. It was hardly a great sacrifice he was making for the company as we were paid next to nothing even at OS rates. I was off the next day, Saturday, on the Adelaide-bound bus.

The trip around the top of the gulf was uneventful and rather boring. We stopped at Maitland on the way and I felt a little pang of guilt thinking of the promise I had made to Barbara.

The wharfies had advised me to stay at the Sailors' Home in the port as it was cheap and well run. There I shared a room with a young Australian seaman possibly a year or two older than myself, who had also booked in that day. We decided to have a look around the port and sort out all its amenities, so off we set on our carousel of the pubs. The old port, halfway up the Torrens river to Adelaide itself, was packed with drinking places nearly next door to each other. Many of these pubs had saloon bars where the local 'good-time girls' were plentiful and friendly to anyone who could buy them a drink. Seafarers were a special attraction to them. This was a truly rollicking sailors' town on a Saturday night.

We met a few keen girls who appealed to us but at that stage we did not arrange any later meetings, meaning to cover the field. At one establishment I got talking to a few Swedish-speaking seamen after hearing them conversing. My new friend wanted to move on and so we parted company expecting to meet up again later. With my new acquaintances I ended up at a pub at the Black Diamond corner.

I was still outside talking to one of them, who was a Finn, while the others had gone into the bar, when of a sudden two men came up behind my companion and grabbed him. He wrestled free, knocked one fellow to the ground and was wrestling with the other one on the pavement and then onto the road. As the first fellow got up I went to engage him as he was going to assist the other one who was underneath the Finn.

But I was grabbed by still another big fellow, slammed against the wall and told I was under arrest. When I protested that I was only going to even up the numbers who had attacked my companion, I was told that they were all police and were going to arrest the Finn on a charge of vagrancy and loitering, now aggravated by assaulting the police, and that if I liked to interfere I could join him.

At that moment my Aussie friend suddenly appeared. He explained to the copper holding me that I was not really with this bunch but was from a ship in Port Victoria, just up in Adelaide for the weekend. He offered to take me back to the Sailors' Home right away.

Watching the Finn being dragged with great difficulty across the road to the port watchhouse around the corner, I gave my name and particulars to the copper who told me to get going and went to assist his associates. At one stage the Finn had them all falling over him in the middle of the traffic even though he was handcuffed. He must have taken some retribution once they got him into the lockup. My friend told me to leave the man to his fate and we went back to the home and to a quiet and early night.

I was about out of money anyway. Later another detective called at the home and interviewed me. Apparently the port was overrun with seamen 'on the beach' who had deserted and were a menace, and the police were going to arrest them all and lock them up till they could be deported. He advised me to get back to my ship and not to associate with them again, for if I was seen in their company I would receive the same treatment.

So much for the Saturday night carousel. Next day I thanked the Aussie for intervening. It was lucky he recognised me as he was passing, as otherwise I may have been convicted and also have received a beating.

I had sent a letter to my uncle to tell him I would meet him on the Monday morning at his son's address, but on the Sunday I was contacted by his son himself, whose name I have since forgotten, and they came down to pick me up from the home. I met the son's wife and we all went out in his car for the rest of the day. I soon realised that my old uncle was a teetotaller and frowned on drinking, smoking and loose women, so I refrained from relating my escapade. He would, I am sure, have had a fit.

We drove up Mount Lofty to the lookout spot overlooking the city of Adelaide. It had certainly been well laid out by Colonel Light, the founder and planner of the city. There it was, like a grid with the river Torrens snaking through the centre, an impressive spectacle. From there we drove up into the Hills and to the Murray river upstream. This was beautiful scenic country, very different from the flat, dry and treeless area around the gulf. We had a picnic at lunchtime and then headed for my hosts' home where we had dinner before they drove me back to the port.

The following day I caught a bus to the city and met my Uncle George in Rundle Street as arranged. He showed me the interesting places around the city, the squares, the churches, the shops, then took me to the zoo and to the Botanical Gardens. Next we went up to Colonel Light's memorial where we had lunch and talked about our families in England and in Australia.

After an afternoon of further sight-seeing, he took me to dinner at the restaurant in the ex-servicemen's club of which he was a member as a veteran from the First World War. On bidding each other goodbye, I promised to write and he promised to send some snaps of the previous day out on to me (neither of which eventuated). And it was back to the Sailor's Home and a quiet night, followed by a last trip to Adelaide early the next morning to catch the bus back to Port Victoria and to work.

*

We were now well into autumn and at times the weather in the Gulf was pretty rough, giving the lumpers and other commuters to and from our vessel an exciting trip out and back ashore. Some came aboard ashen and sick and all wet through with salt water.

We continually renewed our fender lines and the fenders themselves as they wore quickly with the friction of the craft surging alongside against our hull. The feeder vessels generally had double rows of car tyres lashed around outside on their gunwale strakes. Without these tyres and our fenders, the craft would have been stove in and sunk.

Sometimes the sling of bags being loaded was spewed out before it could be lifted fully clear of the feeder when it rose on a high surge. A few bags were lost, although most were saved and recovered by hooks before they sank. It was an art for the hatchman and the winchdriver to anticipate the surge and coordinate the hoisting accordingly.

The increasingly inclement weather sometimes also played havoc with our motorboat's engine and on occasions a trip ashore had to be cancelled leaving 'passengers' stranded either on shore or on board. At night the vessel was left in charge of the night watchman who came on duty at 6pm and stayed on watch till 6am the following morning. All hands in both forecastles who were not occupied at special work took turns at night watchman for seven nights running.

The duties consisted of patrolling the decks from stem to stern. When our 'liberty boat' came alongside he lowered the accommodation ladder and assisted in making it fast securely to the boat boom, which held the craft in place alongside but away from the ship's side. Then he raised the ladder again.

At each hour he had to take a three-point bearing of the shore and the flashing Wauraltee navigation light by using the standard compass. This was to check our position on the chart and see if we had not dragged our anchors and shifted.

Another duty of the night watchman was the cleaning of the galley stove, which meant up-ending all the tops to scrape off all the soot. He then chopped kindling and lighted the fire in time to have boiling coffee ready by 5.30am. He had to call the cooks at 5am and all the rest of the crew with the exception of the master at 5.30am. All started work at 6am, working till breakfast at 8am (or 7.30am for those on cargo work who commenced at 8am).

On two occasions I fell down on this responsible job. The first time I had got nearly through the night, had lit the stove, but then whilst sitting on an upturned bucket in front of the warm fire I nodded off to sleep. I woke up in a heap on the galley deck against the bulkhead with a sickening pain in my side. There was the first mate standing over me and shouting terrible obscenities. He had just woken and realised that he had not been called although it was way past call time.

He tipped over me the bucket of cold water that I had filled to put on the stove for the coffee, hauled me to my feet, ran me out on deck, cuffing me round the ears with terrible threats for my future if I ever repeated such dereliction of responsibility.

The experience was terrifying but not fully effective for I was guilty of another lapse some time later. I knew it was suicidal to sit down inside when feeling dog-tired, but it happened again, and this time before even cleaning or lighting the fire. I woke up under the forecastle head from the cold and from overbalancing at 4am. No galley fire cleaned or kindling lit!

What to do? I hurried to take a bearing and check our position on the chart, did a quick round of the decks and went into the galley to prepare the kindling and get the stove alight. I realised I had no time to clean the stove plates and have the fire blazing and the water boiling for coffee by 5am without some assistance. After the eloquent warning I had had, the fear of a worse penalty than the first time drove me to a desperate and foolish solution. I loaded up the grate with screwed up paper, hastily cut wood and poured kerosene over this. I must have swamped the stove for when I lit a match and threw it in, there was an explosion. The plates jumped inches high and the kindling went everywhere.

What a calamity! I expected everyone to rush in to see what had happened, but with the noise of the wind nobody woke up except the second cook with whom I got on well. When he saw the mess and I explained what had happened, he helped me to put the stove back in order and to light it, this time without kero. Coffee *was* ready at 5.30am. As it happened, the explosion had blasted all the soot off and we had a very clean and glowing stove. But after calling the crew, I made a horrific discovery when doing my last round of the deck. As I came past the galley stack on the midship deck I found it in half. The top part above the stays had been blown off and was lying on the deck full of rents, a crumpled heap of rusted metal. When I called the mate I reported that the galley stack had collapsed from fatigue.

To my relief, the matter was not further investigated and a new top for the stack was made ashore and fitted. I was still very worried, however, as I heard that a story had circulated ashore about a huge ball of flame that had been seen to shoot up from one of the deep-watermen out at anchor, bright enough to illuminate the whole area. Someone had witnessed the event but as all was as usual at daylight the incident was never followed up. I never let on and neither did the cook. It is amazing that the loud explosion was not heard in our adjacent starboard forecastle. Everyone must have been in deep slumber or thought it was a dream.

So providence made me escape retribution on this occasion, and in retrospect the accident even had an amusing conclusion. But I swore never again to sit down in any comfort when I took up the night watch after a day's work or not having had a proper sleep recently.

*

The first to finish loading was the *Lawhill*. She had arrived first and so had priority of service from the grain sheds and farms as well as the feeder craft. One mid-morning we faintly heard the continuous ringing of a ship's bell and understood it was marking the final sling of cargo being loaded onto the *Lawhill*. We knew that this occasion was imminent as she was down to her marks and we sympathised with the excitement such events always provoke on board a cargo vessel. Hopefully, it would soon be our turn to be homeward bound.

Early next morning we heard the bell again as her first anchor came free of the bottom. She was on the regular run across the Indian Ocean, so this departure would have been a minor event for her crew, who would be home in a few weeks at the most. Our own voyage, however, would take months. After lunch the bell sounded again and when we looked she was under way with all her fore-and-afters and topsails set. The breeze was off the land and soon we saw her lads freeing her topgallants. By the time she came abreast of us she had these all sheeted home.

She crossed no royals. The *Lawhill*, a heavy utility carrier built by Britain in the 1890s, had been designed to achieve labour saving on board and engaged smaller crews to handle the larger sail areas. So royals were out and Jarvis bracing winches were fitted as well as halyard winches for the lower yards. She was also unique in that she stepped her topmasts and topgallant masts on the after side of the lower ones at the doublings. This innovation was probably not particularly successful as it was only ever tried on one other Hill Line vessel.

We were now down to two, the *Viking* by this time being over half loaded. Our feeder boat visits increased and sometimes we received two on the same day, at which occasion a second gang of lumpers came out with the schooner to work the second hatch. As we went down on our marks it came to the dreaded time to move out to the ballast grounds where we dumped on the bottom of the gulf the sand and rock we had loaded in Malaya.

This meant ten days out of our cargo loading and eight days' hard grind, working twelve hours a shift. I don't think anyone from forward went ashore during this period.

Work, that is day work, started at 6am after coffee. We had two meal breaks of thirty minutes during this twelve-hour time. There were also two coffee breaks but these were spelling breaks and work continued.

We shovelled the ballast into bins or heavy wicker baskets that were hoisted out of the hatches with the help of the winches. The hardest part was to start a new layer, when we had to dig down into the compacted material then lift our shovelful the whole height of the receptacle.

As the material went out it left an ever-growing hole into which the receptacle could be placed at various positions around the rim, making it easier to fill, until at the bottom a final exertion was needed in shovelling upwards. A mixture of sand and stone was one of the worst materials to handle as one's shovel kept jarringly striking rocks. The bigger rocks had to be dug out and lifted into the basket by hand.

By dusk you climbed up out the hold, staggered down the deck black with dirt and sweat caked on your body, and cursing the day you had decided to go to sea. After a preliminary wash-off in salt water, you had a thorough wash in fresh water with soap, then ate your meal mindlessly and immediately went to sleep to replenish your energy for the next day's labour.

This was unfortunately one of the frequent chores on board sailing vessels. When tempted by nostalgic regrets for the days of sail, one should give a thought to the countless young sailors lured to sea by dreams of exotic adventures who have found themselves digging ballast for weeks down stifling holds, hell holes in summer everywhere, and in the tropics almost unbearable.

Our friends on the *Viking* were spared this purgatory. She had a double bottom and used water ballast.

We shifted back to our loading point after waiting for a wind from the right direction, and we anchored further in to the position where the *Lawhill* had loaded and nearer to the wharf, which made a shorter run for the feeders.

A diversion from our now boring round of work routine was soon afforded us with the completion of the *Viking*'s cargo. The night before we had gone ashore and met her crew who were having a last fling, so we were ready for their departure. We watched the last of the bags of grain come out to the *Viking* and then stores for her voyage home to Europe via Falmouth. By mid-morning we heard the bell sounding as her first anchor cleared off the bottom, then further strikes of the bell as the second cable was shortened up.

While working, we kept an eye on the activity on her board. There was movement aloft as her yards were trimmed so that she would fall off correctly to the prevailing wind on freeing her final anchor. Topsails and topgallants were loosed ready to top and sheet home and her motor 'liberty boat' was heaved up and turned in. In the afternoon we heard the bell ringing in her final sling of bags and soon after it was sounding again as the second anchor came free from the bottom. We all stopped work and gathered to watch her departure. The agent's boat left her side and her topsails and fore-and-aft headsails pushed her around to the heading she had to take to clear us and then pick up her departure course.

Soon she was abreast of us and we gave her a farewell cheer and wave with the feeling that we would not be too long behind her and might even, if we were lucky, catch her up. How little did we realise, as she passed setting sail after sail, that we would not see her again.

The *Viking* was now in fact on her last commercial voyage. The day was 11th March. She had a long if uneventful run of 139 days to Falmouth via the

Horn. In Falmouth she got orders to discharge in Millwall's West India Dock, after which there was a possibility of her becoming once again a training ship, this time for Sweden. But this fell through as the Swedes decided she was too big and expensive to run and bought the topsail schooner *Sunbeam* instead. So with no work in the offing Edgar Erikson sent her over to lay up at Antwerp, as Holland had indicated some interest. But in the end the city of Gothenburg bought her. In 1951 she sailed to that city and became a stationary navigation school and hostel. There she has remained till this day.

As for us, our predicted departure by the end of the month was never achieved. Even though we had the services of the three feeders and two gangs of lumpers, all came to an sudden stop when a severe storm swept in from the SW across South Australia and into Victoria, causing much disruption and considerable damage. After the second day of fully operational stevedoring the wind and the rising sea and swell made it unsafe for the feeders to stay alongside. Both cast off with what cargo they had left in them and headed for their lay-up wharf for fear of being damaged against our hull even with extra fenders.

That night the weather deteriorated and it blew a hurricane. Our anchor cables were stretched taut and at times we could feel our vessel drag then come up as the anchors bit and held again. The sea almost broke over the bow and sent continuous sheets of spray over the decks. All through that day and well into the night we put our faith in the anchors holding us from grounding or worse.

By the next morning the worst had passed and sea and wind were moderating. We were told that we had dragged a fair way but were still in deep enough waters to finish loading without having to reposition. However when we looked to the shore and the feeder wharf no craft could be seen. Next we heard on the 'galley grapevine', from the Old Man who heard the news on his wireless receiver, to the steward who passed it to the cook who told us, that the storm had lifted many roofs off houses in Adelaide and other centres and had sunk many small craft.

Another day went by and then, with only a breeze but still a swell, came a launch out with our agent and the bad news. The storm had sunk the two feeders that had cast off from us. They returned to the lay-up wharf only to be holed alongside during the first night of the storm and they were now on the bottom. The third feeder, a ketch, had slipped out to take refuge at anchor on the lee of the island and was safe. No work was expected for a while, so we took the opportunity to get ashore to see the damage and talk to our mates who had all got ashore when the feeders sank.

It was a sad sight. The beautiful three-mast schooner and the three-mast ketch were on the bottom with only their topmasts free of the surface. It was decided to attempt to salvage them both and divers came from Port Adelaide as well as salvage and pumping equipment including air pumps.

Some of the burst and swollen bags of grain had first to be taken out of their hulls before the pressure on their already fractured timbers caused more damage. Then the divers inserted air bags into the holds and accommodation spaces, blocked off holes and openings with rubber sheeting and air was pumped into the bags while water was pumped out. It was quite a contest which went on for several days and which we watched with interest when we had shore leave. At last the schooner broke the surface. The crew went into the hold and after hours of herculean effort discharged the remaining swollen bags back onto the wharf.

The gear was shifted to the second craft and the same procedure used to bring that one to the surface too. They were both made ready with temporary repairs, and about two weeks after the sinking set out on a hazardous trip out of Spencer Gulf and over Gulf St Vincent to the slipway in Port Adelaide for lasting repairs.

Storm damage had also occurred inland. The roofs of some farm grain sheds had been lifted causing the grain ready to be sent to town to be condemned for export. This meant that the amount of bags coming down to the wharf was reduced and only supplied the third ketch that had escaped being sunk or damaged by its prompt 'safety first' intuition of running for cover.

During this period of delay we did maintenance work and prepared for our forthcoming long voyage, the most eventful task being the sending up and recrossing of the royal yards after repairing and renewing their fittings and painting them.

Loading, after some time, settled down to a regular pattern again, and towards the end of April we were back to two feeders, a second ketch joining us with a second gang of lumpers. We now realised that it would be May before departure and therefore winter when rounding the Horn. We were told however that the consolation for the winter weather voyage was that we would not encounter icebergs as they only break free and drift north in the summer.

We were at this time only a skeleton crew, for more had either paid off or disappeared. The second and third mates had gone back to the *Viking* and had sailed with her. Stag Siren, a Swedish Finn, had somehow managed to induce the master to pay him off, and of the others that left, I presumed they jumped ship.

In the last week before leaving, new hands began to join us. Most were South Australians, some from other states and two from England. One of these, Dainty Moore, was a naval Lieutenant Commander who had taken leave and signed on for the run home for the experience. The other, Tom Owens, was a seaman from Liverpool choosing an unusual way home. One of the Aussies, Bill Hillwood, signed as AB having done a round trip before the war in the *Archibald Russel*. A new Aussie chief cook joined as did a mess-boy. Then came the others one by one, although we had to wait a few days after loading was completed for the final number to make up the complement.

I took the opportunity of these extensive changes to try my luck again and approach the captain with a request for promotion, and this time he finally agreed to make me an OS. I do not remember having signed new articles at the time, but I got the pay and the status.

The four hatches were battened down and covered with their planking, which had been stowed aside. They were lashed for heavy weather with wire hove tight on bottle screws. We took aboard stores of provisions, kerosene, cordage, wood and coal for the bogies in our forecastles and the officers' cabins. Oilskins and sea boots were got out and recoated for the expected heavy use. Sails, all heavy weather, were bent and running gear overhauled.

Lastly the master had to appoint his mates in accordance with the Australian Navigation Act which required at least a certified mate for each watch. We only had the first mate and himself left aboard, so Mike Ruffhead's second mate ticket was used for the record. But he was really our sailmaker and of course a day worker. Our donkeyman Marti Suomi was therefore appointed the acting second mate and Franz Forsman, our chippy, became the third mate, to stand watch with the first mate. Ingvar Sundquist was promoted to the chippy's job and Elmer Egblom to the donkeyman's job.

After ten long weeks in Port Victoria, fully loaded with 59,000 bags of grain, we were at last ready to sail and complete the Great Circle.

Chapter 9

HOMEWARD BOUND VIA THE HORN

We sailed on 17th May 1948. We had been eagerly waiting for this day, especially those of us still left from the group who had joined in Finland. That event seemed ages away now. However memories and thoughts were put aside in the bustle of preparation for departure. We made an upsetting discovery at this moment: the fresh water we had taken aboard from the lighter to fill our two tanks had a very nasty taste. And yet we had cleaned the tanks after they had been emptied of the water taken in Malaya and we had lime-washed the interior surfaces. Although South Australian water was never the best this was brackish to the extreme and would have been rejected on other ships. We were now stuck with it and would have to smother its taste in our drinking ration with coffee or lime juice until we could dilute it by mixing it with the rainwater we caught at the earliest opportunity.

The donkey engine, now under the command of Elmer Egblom, was started well before breakfast and we connected up the endless wire driving line from the engine barrel forward to the barrel on the windlass, five turns on each barrel. We put the windlass into gear and as the brake on the gipsy was released the donkey barrel was engaged by Elmer and to a rousing cheer the gipsy started to turn, bringing up the first anchor link by link.

Two men went down the chain locker to stow the chain neatly as it came in. The locker men were all new hands, with the exception of ABs or OSs of course. By mid-morning the anchor was hove to and catted, ready to be dropped again if necessary. The other cable was hove up short but we left the second anchor still embedded in the bottom and the cable nearly straight up and down while all hands had their meal including the relieved locker men.

A fair breeze was coming off the shore and was expected to strengthen and then back to the north. The agent and other visitors at last departed in the shore launch. Ours had been turned inboard and secured the previous day as no shore leave was ever given the night before sailing. We had said our farewells to the ketch's crew and to our local friends on our final fling ashore before sailing eve. The accommodation ladder was raised, unfitted, brought inboard and stowed on the midship deck, lashed securely out of the way of heavy seas. Our after ladder was securely slung under the catwalk aft, again out of the usual reach of the sea.

At noon a few of us went up to throw off the gaskets of all the lower square sails including the lower topgallants but with the exception of the main and cro'jack. Inner headsails were hoisted and spanker gaffs and jigger staysails readied to set. Braces were cleared ready to be run and heaved on.

Next was the sort-out of the new hands and we all assembled at the after end of the foredeck, those of the previous watches on their respective sides, the new hands in the middle. The mate and the new second mate picked the balance into their watches. This meant some new members changing forecastles, but as none had a lot of gear and possessions this was done in no time at all.

At last the donkey engine which had been kept idling was engaged again and the second anchor was hove up to the pipe and left there ready to drop again if necessary. We were under way.

Our donkey engine had done a magnificent job. Elmer had meticulously overhauled and tested it and it functioned beautifully on the day for this mammoth task. The alternative was too horrible to contemplate after our experience off Cape Town when we had to bring in our anchor by hand. This time, with two anchors down, the job would have taken all day with the whole crew taking turns trudging round the capstan.

Our head fell off to the breeze and round she came with the help of the head-sails which were sheeted home on the side she had headed. One man went to the wheel which was put over till ready to steady on our departure course. Meanwhile the other hands had manned the upper topsail halyard winches, topped all three yards and were now sheeting home all these square sails one after the other. The yards were then trimmed to comply with the course and wind. Most tasks went smoothly considering that half the crew were new hands, us 'old' hands excelling in showing these how things were done.

Gradually in the breeze and under this spread of sail she gained momentum and came round to head for the outlet from the Gulf for easterly bound traffic. Our own course was to round Kangaroo Island instead of going through the Backstairs Passage.

The three top men went up again to free the upper topgallants and the newly bent royals. These yards were soon topped, the sails sheeted home and yards trimmed. We coiled the gaskets while the others set the rest of the fore-and-afters. Our watch was on from 1pm to 7pm, but it was only after 3pm that the port watch was able to go below. The job left to us was to square up the deck, coil all the lines, then check all moveable objects which were diligently lashed down, as we knew too well the consequences of gear breaking loose in heavy weather.

By midnight when we came on watch again, the breeze had fallen away to light airs and we had only covered seven miles in five hours. In the following morning watch, 8am to 1pm, we sent down the main upper topsail and bent a newer and stronger one.

In the afternoon the port watch catted the second anchor then brought them both on deck with the crane. After the chains were stowed in the lockers the sealing of the spurling pipes was done meticulously. We remembered the near tragedy experienced in the north Atlantic when the loss of the spurling pipes' plugs and the vent plugs had allowed the flooding of the forepeak via the chain lockers and almost caused the demise of the vessel. The two anchors were bolted down on their deck housings with extra chain lashings. While all this labour was in progress our watch had its six hours off below.

That evening when we were again on watch we picked up Cape Border light on our port side and far away on the horizon to starboard was the faint loom of what we reckoned was South Neptune light. At eight bells and change of watch we wore ship to pick up the westerlies. Before we went below we spoke by Morse, using a torch, to the SS *Barwon* that was heading east and passed close by our stern.

Next day the crane was lifted out of its base by a tackle off the forestay and also lashed securely on the forecastle head. Lifelines were stretched both sides the full length of both well decks and three-foot high nets were rigged above the gunwales each side aft of the foremast backstays and aft of the mizzen mast backstays. We were as ready as we could possibly be for any challenge.

At last we were clear of Kangaroo Island and headed SSW to make around 46 degrees south before we squared away with the prevailing westerlies on an ESE course that would take us well south of Tasmania and across the Tasman. We were then to pass between the Snares (rock islands) and Auckland Islands well south of New Zealand.

'Running the easting down', as it was called (sailing east towards the Greenwich meridian) was a long-suffering exercise. Because of our bad luck with the westerlies and the captain's decision not to carry the normal amount of sail when the wind was favourable, constant and strong, it took us 19 days to reach the International Date Line on Saturday 5th June. On that occasion we took heart in enjoying two Saturdays with the 1pm general work finish.

The Roaring Forties gave way as we made southing to the 'Filthy' Fifties. This course, we hoped, would take us well south of Cape Horn but still north of the winter polar ice cap.

The route we were taking complied with the navigation method which was used on most sailing ships built around the early 1900s. This method, known as Great Circle sailing, had been introduced rather recently, around 1850. It was based on a theory developed by United States Navy Lieutenant Matthew Maury. An expert in oceanography, he had collated a mass of meteorological data around the globe and advocated the use of favourable winds and currents, according to seasons, to determine the speediest sailing courses. Going the long way on a voyage is often the quickest way when one is dependent on the winds. Maury's suggested Great Circle route for the run out from Europe to Australia or New Zealand consisted of taking advantage of the NE trade winds down to Cape São Roque off Brazil, then going on the opposite tack and beating a SSE course in the SE trades till well south of the latitude of the Cape of Good Hope, and then squaring away on picking up the westerlies and sailing well down into the Roaring Forties across the southern ocean, till finally heading NW to make landfall either in Australia or New Zealand.

From there, instead of the traditional return route via the Indian Ocean, Maury recommended the route east, via Cape Horn, using the prevailing westerlies across the southern ocean. Vessels which tried out his theory proved him correct and managed to cut the voyage time considerably. This caused a new building boom for sailing ships now using iron and steel construction. It could be said that Matthew Maury promoted the last great era of sail.

Following this route, however, meant heavy-weather sailing, for it must be realised that in the latitudes below 45° S the west wind prevails throughout the year and except for the barrier of the bottom of South America no land mass stands in its path. Ten degrees further south there is no impediment at all and the effect of this wind force upon the ocean surface is severe in the extreme. The height of the waves down there and the distance between their crests are enormous. They are the 'greybeards', the world's biggest.

Sailing from east to west against these seas and wind was the supreme challenge for sailors at any time of the year. Most casualties in the history of rounding the Horn happened to vessels beating westward before they could chance bearing away north up the Chilean coast or NE into the Pacific. Earlier sailing vessels which were comparatively small and made of wood (with the exception of the Yankee Down Easters, some of which were 3,000-ton vessels) were the toys of the forces of nature meted out there. But even the larger steel-built vessels, which rode lower with less freeboard than wooden vessels, had considerable difficulty rounding the Horn westward and many were also posted missing.

Slowly clawing westward, mainly by wearing ship (as in such wind velocity tacking was suicide), it often took days and even weeks before a master could be confident of his position and dare to fall away north. Many gave up after battling a lost cause, continuously being carried back to where they commenced the combat. Some went for shelter or for repairs in the Falkland Islands but most turned and squared away, often damaged, their provisions almost exhausted and their crew beaten and injured. They ran before their tormentor the west wind, easted across the southern ocean and came up to the Chilean coast sometimes 200 and more days out from Europe having circumnavigated the globe.

Taking the Great Circle route eastward, as we did, was less of a challenge, since the wind was favourable, but the heavy seas still made any voyage in these latitudes a daunting experience. Many vessels were dismasted and many foundered rounding the Horn even by this 'easy way'.

These turbulent latitudes presented other dangers as well. In winter there was very little daylight, snow and sleet squalls were numerous, and the temperature and wind-chill numbing. Wind strength was at times of hurricane force and the seas consequently very bad. These extreme conditions made all sailing tasks such as tacking, wearing, even bracing, very dangerous exercises as seas filled the well decks continuously like rolling swimming pools.

Hands were washed under and carried across the deck to come up against the bulwarks or hatch coamings. If still capable of movement, the self-preservation instinct generally gave the victim the impulse to grab a lifeline or some other object and haul himself above the raging seas. If he was hurt or knocked unconscious others, when the chance came, would haul him to safety and lash him until the job was completed and he could be carried aft for treatment.

On many voyages men were plucked from the line they were attending and washed over the side. Some unfortunate vessels lost nearly the whole watch overboard this way. There are accounts of hands being washed over but then miraculously flung back inboard by the next oncoming wave. But in most cases being washed overboard meant drowning, as no sailing ship in such weather could heave to, let alone launch a lifeboat to look for the victim. To attempt a rescue in these conditions would have been a foolish act of heroism meaning the almost certain loss of the boat's crew, and probably of the vessel itself. All that could be done was to throw a life buoy over and pray for the sailor's soul. In fact, throwing a buoy was not even necessarily the most charitable thing to do, for really, if the victim were lucky enough to grab it, that would only have prolonged his suffering. In such circumstances and in such remote regions he could never have been found.

A much feared occurrence when running before the wind in these huge seas was a 'pooping'. An exceptionally massive greybeard would build up its crest so high that the vessel had no time to raise its stern high and quickly enough for it to ride the wave passing under it. The wave would bury the vessel from the poop and roll forward taking with it all that it could prise loose, often leaving a deck stripped bare to the forecastle break, in the case of a full-length well decker, even sweeping away the whole watch on deck including the mate, the helmsmen, along with the wheel and box, chartroom, lifeboats, deckhouses and fittings. Even if only the helmsman was swept from the after wheel on being pooped, this had catastrophic consequences as the vessel would inevitably broach to, having no one to steer it over the next wave. It is believed that many vessels posted missing in these latitudes were lost in such circumstances.

It became known from survivors that some vessels suffered disastrous damage through broaching without actually being pooped and it was suspected that this may have been due to fear. It is quite possible that on glancing over their shoulder the helmsmen had been so horrified at seeing a massive wave towering up behind them that they had lost their nerve and abandoned the wheel in an attempt to escape their fate by running forward or jumping into the after-mast rigging.

To prevent this most often fatal casualty several of the later-built sailing vessels had a steel cover, called a whaleback, erected over the wheel. This protected the helmsmen and the watch officer in the event of a pooping and allowed them to stay in control of the vessel. It also prevented the helmsmen from seeing what was building up behind them. The same protection was achieved when the German architects had the idea, soon imitated by others, of building midship sections on top of which the main steering wheel was placed and which broke the forward sweep of any but the largest poop waves. The *Passat* was built on this design.

Many ships were lucky and never had trouble on the voyages they made rounding the Horn or even doubling it on the one voyage. From the 1900s, the large heavily built nitrate carriers of France and Germany made three and even four roundings of this infamous Cape in the year without any loss or serious incident and it seemed these well fitted out, expertly sailed and navigated ships had at last mastered the fury of Cape Horn before the era of sail came to an end.

We fortunately did not suffer any dramatic incidents on this voyage, but we had our share of very heavy weather which tested our nerves and physical resistance to the full.

Any work aloft, mainly at reducing sail, repairing a torn sail or replacing a blown-out one, was a supreme effort. Just reaching the yard to furl a sail and making it out on a footrope left one gasping. Then came the battle to smother the iced iron-stiff canvas, bellied out before one by an 80-mile-per-hour wind often full of sleet, and the laborious work of rolling it up on the yard with numb hands and lashing it with double gaskets so it would not be blown free. To do this job under the threat that the canvas was going to be blown to shreds any minute was a terrible experience that left one totally fatigued. Especially if there was more than one sail to combat. Then a whole watch below could be spent at this task. And after such a tremendous effort the lines still had to be cleared from the deck and coiled up on the stays above the pin-rails as far out of reach of the surging mass of sea as possible.

On a couple of occasions, when all hands had been giving their most for twelve hours, a tot of brandy was allowed by our master and dished out by the mate. When eventually we got to our forecastle we shed our oilskins and collapsed fully clothed into our bunks and the sleep of the dead after one prayer, that we would not be called out again in the next four hours.

Life in the two forecastles was rough in the extreme under these conditions. The doors out onto the forward well deck were closed permanently and the dogs hammered down on them. This meant that the only access in or out of our quarters was through the skylight hatch above the mess table, which opened onto the midship deck. As the cover of the skylight was closed unless being used for access, and the portholes of course were dogged down with their deadlights, the air in the forecastle was most foul. This predicament was exacerbated by the bogey heater which often produced billows of smoke from the wet firewood used.

Despite all efforts to keep the seas out water still leaked into our domain and after a while a few inches' depth of sea water would be constantly washing back and forth to add to our discomfort. A week on from rounding the south of New Zealand no one had any dry clothes and even our blankets were wet from us turning into our bunks almost fully dressed. By the time we had thawed out under the damp blankets and started to dry these out with our body's heat we got called and had to abandon our temporary snugness, to put our sea-boots and oilskins on, grab a mug of coffee or a meal and struggle through the skylight onto the freezing deck ready to brave the elements at the wheel, lookout or any other job that had been held back for the change of the watch. No one bothered to make any unnecessary conversation. Body and nerves were stretched but as we were most often groggy with fatigue the necessity for sleep and recuperation blocked out the realisation of our privation.

This had been the lot of the seafarers who, voyage after voyage, manned the vessels sailing in these regions over the centuries. In the short summer months the elements were not so cruel. The days were longer and the temperature milder, but in the main the wind and seas were the same, without the sleet and snow. The special danger of the summer was the risk of collision with the icebergs that break off from the iceshelf in the warmer temperature and drift north.

In this season lookouts were posted at all times. Sailing ships were always at greater risk than steamships owing to the difficulty of suddenly changing course

The *Passat* loading timber in Kotka, October 1946.

The *Passat's* British apprentices. Clockwise: Max Wood, (wearing cap), Terry Dwyer, Martin Lee, Bob Deacon (who joined in South Africa) and Adrian Small.

'Yanny' (Hans Hongel) belaying a line on the pin rail.

Passat under full sail in the Channel, braced hard on the stays.

Marti Suomi, donkeyman.

South Africa, 1947. Black convicts working on the wharf.

Beating into Bunbury, Western Australia

Leaving Bunbury for Malaya. Sailing out of port, fully laden and without tugs.

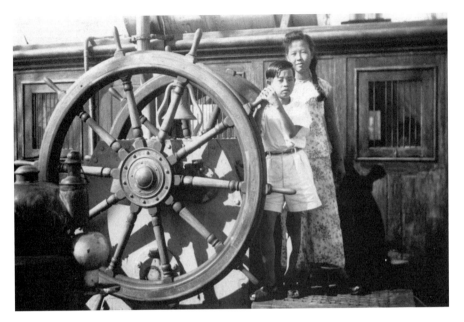

In Port Swettenham, the author's Chinese friends from the shop visit the *Passat*.

Max steering at the after wheel on the run to Cape Horn.

Man relashing a gasket on the foreyard, while heading for the Horn.

The *Passat* laid up as a stationery training ship in Travemünde, Germany, 1989.

under sail or of coming to a halt in heavy seas and strong winds. Many ships posted overdue and missing were thought to have been unable to avoid a collision with a berg.

On our winter passage the lookout was kept from dusk to dawn which meant, at that time of the year, about 16 hours per day, more if visibility was reduced and the mate of the watch decided a lookout was necessary during the day, for instance in fog. Although high winds were experienced for most of the passage, there were occasions when the wind would fall away for a while and leave the vessel wallowing and becalmed in the huge swell. Fog could envelop the area in such conditions. There were also occasions when the skies cleared and visibility improved, allowing the sighting of the Cape itself.

The lookout's position was on the forecastle head. It was a pleasant duty in fair weather when you could walk up and down while scanning the horizon. But in heavy weather you had to hang on to the forestay or some other solid support so as not to be flung or washed off your exposed position if the bow decided to go through the crest of a wave and not over it. In most cases seas were not directly ahead unless when the wind shifted from the direction it had caused the sea to run. But when running close-hauled the sea was on the bow and would often keep a lookout drenched for the whole of his trick. Your lookout turn could be a miserable time, especially if sailing work commenced and your relief was engaged in such occupation; then you had to stay at your post for long hours until relieved.

The lookout's duty was to report any light or object he saw by sounding the forward bell, one strike for starboard, two for port and three strikes for right ahead. When that happened if the mate of the watch could not identify the sighting from amidships, or on a flush-decker from the poop, he would come forward or send another watch keeper forward to have the sighting pointed out.

In the shipping lanes of steamships it was common to see a light, or when near land even to report the land itself in moonlight or in star-lit nights. But in the run across the southern ocean no such sightings could be expected except for an occasional coastal steamer around Tierra Del Fuego. Very few ships ever came down to such latitudes except whalers and some fishing vessels.

It was also quite rare to encounter another sailing ship in these regions after the Second World War. It was in fact nigh impossible to sight a sailing ship's sidelights unless quite near and in moderate weather and with fair visibility. It was nevertheless also the duty of the lookout to observe periodically that the sidelights were burning and could be seen. If either one was not in order he had to report it to the mate who would get that light attended to, cleaned and relit. When relieved, the lookout inspected the lights and, on reporting to the mate of the watch, said the lights were 'burning bright'.

Another function of the lookout in conditions of very bad visibility was to fetch the hand-operated fog horn from under the forecastle, set it up and sound it every three minutes, one blast for the starboard tack, two for port tack and three when running free. Incidentally, this apparatus was also used in summer when visibility was poor and a sudden fall of the temperature was noticed suggesting the possible proximity of an iceberg: the return of an echo would have indicated that the obstacle was close.

*

Apart from times of danger when concentration was needed, I found lookout duties a relaxing time when my mind was free to wander off. On this voyage home my head was teeming with reflections about the past and with plans and dreams for the future that would open for me when we docked at our discharge port and eventually paid off articles. It seemed ages to me since I had left London to join the *Passat* and so much had taken place in my life!

Most in my mind at the time was the change that had occurred in my family's circumstances and how I was to adapt to the new situation.

Until now I had not been prone to meditate about my own life, but what for the effects of my long absence, the maturation I had undergone during these two years, and the dramatic events that had unfolded at home, I found myself going insistently over the story of my childhood.

This story was unfortunately dominated, shall I say overshadowed, by the figure of my father. He was a tyrant, and at the same time a weak man who vented his wrath on vulnerable people. He would never engage anyone who could retaliate and was careful with other men. He was a wife and child beater at home but a saint when in public. Because I was a boy I was spared to some degree the vicious treatment he inflicted on my mother and sister. I am sure now that he was born with such an attitude to others as his brothers and sisters were never like him. His father was however a weak character and took refuge in drink. His mother ran the household and she was the one he feared.

At 17 he went off to the First World War and served in France and Belgium throughout the campaigns. After the armistice he stayed on in the army as a sergeant during the occupation of the Rhine. He used to boast about his war years and to try and sicken us with vivid descriptions of wounded and dying men and rotting corpses. He was only lightly wounded by shrapnel himself. His other boast was how he sold army stores on the German black market after 1918.

When he was at last discharged he came back to London and passed an entry exam into the Civil Service. He entered the Customs and Excise department in the docks, I suppose because his home was near the Royal Docks. He then met and charmed my mother who was naive, trusting and romantic. She married him against all advice from her family who could see through his facade.

Soon, in 1926, my sister Joyce was born but he never showed much affection for her. For him she was only another female. About 1929 after doing well in the customs and passing exams he was transferred to Harwich docks. This was the main ferry port to the Hook of Holland. In 1930 I was born. Like my sister I had olive skin, and brown hair and eyes. He was himself blue eyed, fair skinned with ginger hair and my mother had olive skin, blue eyes but dark hair. He accused her of infidelity and from then on his treatment of her got even worse.

A few months after my birth he was transferred to a desk job and soon after he went back to the London docks again but in a higher position. During this time he was playing around while Mum was forced to beg from her family to feed us and keep house. He never took us on any holiday but he himself was going more and more frequently to Germany on his holidays. Soon he proclaimed he was an admirer of Hitler and that the Nazis were his ideal.

We had from then on to put up with his propaganda. Although he supported the Fascists under Mosley in Britain, he never actually joined them. They engaged in fighting with other men and as I have said he was really a coward. He was also too cunning to risk losing his job and compromising his future by committing himself publicly. What if they were to be on the losing side?

So we were brought up on anti-semitism and the worship of the pure Aryan values, whatever these were. This all caused great upset in my grandparents' home as my father's philosophy was vehemently opposed by his younger brother, and shouting matches developed often, ending with my grandmother ordering my father out of her house.

We really never were won over to his tirades. He was a fierce anti-communist of course as well as anti-trade union. The great depression never gave my father any compassion for any of those all around us. He had a safe permanent job and although he never allowed my mother enough to live on, he lived well and we had a roof over our heads and food. So we were better off than most of my school mates.

I believe around 1936 he went to some of the big Fascist rallies held at Earls Court. About a year after this, he was transferred away from shipping to the excise department of Imperial Airways, at Croydon aerodrome, south of London. Here he became middle class and we moved to a middle-class area near the aerodrome where he put a deposit on a semi-detached modern house on a new estate. The trips to Germany were easier for him now as he flew by plane.

My sister and I attended the local council school and my mother battled on as the uncomplaining suburban housewife trying to keep up appearances on what she could beg and what little he allowed us. My father of course was now able to put on a phoney appearance and to neighbours he was a nice decent office worker always gracious and neatly attired. At one time he even conned a car from some rich woman he was running around with and we had the only car in the street parked outside whenever he was home.

Then came the outbreak of war and Joyce and I were evacuated with most of our school to East Grinstead, a country town in Sussex twenty or so miles south of London. My mother at last got out of his clutches to a degree owing to the war. Relieved of the daily care of her children, she applied for war work and, having had experience at secretarial work before her marriage, she became in time a secretary in the Air Ministry to one of the top air commanders, travelling each day to the City.

Croydon aerodrome was closed down after being bombed in the early 'phoney' part of the war. It was an obvious target as Lufthansa used it on a daily basis before the war. The raid was led by the prior senior German civil air pilot and so the landing strips, tarmac and hangars were easily destroyed.

Thereafter my father was switched to another civil service department and he also travelled to the City each day. It was, I realise now, his cunning that had kept him clear of the authorities, but he was also very lucky not to have been rounded up and interned for the duration of the war. As it was, he ended up as sergeant again, this time in the home guard.

I stayed in East Grinstead from 1939 to early 1942. I had during this time several billets for different lengths of time but I was never with my sister: boys and girls were foolishly separated and yet would be billeted in homes that had children of the opposite sex. My last billet was for the longest period, over a year, and with a kind family, the Edwards. They had a son, Michael, a bit younger than myself. At last I had found a place where I was looked after and liked as if I was a second son. I was very content there and for the first time enjoyed a happy family atmosphere.

Alas at the beginning of 1943 as the London Blitz was over it was decided to send us home. So Joyce and I came back to Croydon and to living under fear and tension again. My father became even more aggressive towards my mother and sister who was always in trouble even though she was by then 17 and had left school. One day, after he had bashed her badly, she went to stay at a friend's home while I was packed off to my grandparents' place in East Ham. When I eventually came back to Croydon I found that Joyce had left to join the army and was in the Transport section driving lorries.

I was growing up fast and by 1944 was starting to test my father's authority while still frightened of his fast and hard physical punishment. However a new *modus vivendi* was attained as a result of my reaction to a brutal attack he made in my presence on my mother who had dared to disagree with him. He had punched her and then kicked her and was going to do more damage. I lost all fear and rushed at him punching wildly with no thought of the likely severe retaliation. I told him that if he hit my mother again I would get my gang to beat him up. I did belong to a gang of youths, some of whom, being around 17 years, were pretty tough characters, even carrying and using at times knuckle-dusters. Confronted with this outburst his tactics changed from then on. He warned me that if I interfered again in his administration of discipline he would have me sent to Borstal (a boys' prison home). I knew I had won a victory though and said that my threat stood and I did not worry at such a future.

By this time the flying bombs had started, and it was a big diversion from normal life in our area. Croydon had the honour of receiving more of these bombs than any other borough. Three landed in our street, damaging most houses and taking the roof, doors and windows out of our own. Two of them landed in the daytime and I watched them coming until the engines cut out and they started their silent downward glide, at which time I dived for cover under our Morrison shelter in the living room. This was a box erected in the house, as high as a table and used as such, with steel top, bottom and corner angles, and with wire mesh sides, one of them left open for access.

This crisis interrupting daily life continued into 1945 until the air and ground defences reorganised and succeeded in shielding the south of England. From then on, the majority of V1s were shot down before getting far over the Channel. Then the advancing Allied forces overran the German launching bases, and after we had received a few last V2s, the danger from the air was over. My father would have by now realised that his ideological champions were going to lose the war, a thought that, no doubt, made him even more morose.

When V-day came and the street, town and country all celebrated, my father took no part. My sister was eventually demobilised and enrolled for an education course that was offered to any members of the defence forces willing to take advantage of it. They were subsidised with a living allowance as well under the new Labour government. Here she met her future husband who was also doing a course. She never came back to what was left of home.

I soon left home too. Realising that I had become a threat to his way of life, and that I would soon be coming up 16 in age anyway and be able to do as I pleased, my father finally agreed to let me go to sea, as long as I was apprenticed.

After I joined the *Passat* I suspect he might have been relieved in a way at the thought that he could reign supreme over my mother. Joyce realised this too and managed to convince Mum that she no longer had a pressing reason for staying in this household as her duty of providing a home for her children was completed.

I no longer felt resentment at my mother's desertion. I sympathised with her feelings and approved her action. But it felt as if my childhood was lost for ever. It belonged to another world, now inaccessible. 'Coming home' had lost much of its meaning for me.

I would now be on my own and would have to find my own accommodation. I knew I would have to obtain work urgently as the pittance I paid off with would not last for more than a few weeks. And I had to consider what would be the best course if I wanted to pursue a career at sea. Such thoughts occupied my time on lookout for the rest of the voyage.

*

Our navigation methods, as I explained earlier, were very basic and owing to the lack of modern instruments it was an accomplishment of our master and his assistants that we arrived off Cape Horn, rounded it, and sailed on into the Atlantic without slamming into the Chilean coast. We would not have been the first to have ended up that way. Such voyages were indeed always fraught with danger as navigation when running the easting down was often very erratic. While sailing in these conditions put great strain on crews, it will be realised that masters, on their part, were under considerable stress in these latitudes where the elements often made the use of their basic navigational aids impossible for long periods.

To illustrate the constant vigilance and hardwork required of a crew in the vicinity of Cape Horn, even on a relatively trouble-free passage, I can do no better than to reproduce here a few pages from my personal logbook.

Friday 25th June 41 days out. No position.
Course ENE ½ E. Wind west. Strong snow squalls. Cold. Port watch sent down the mizzen lower topsail in the forenoon watch. We with their initial help bent a brand new sail in place. Mike and self were out on the port yardarm for 3 hours shackling on the sheet and the clew line, as we had several twists in the leech. The sail was not set. We also put new rovings on the foresail of which about 8ft of the bunt had come adrift. A big sea came over the midships while Martin and I were at the wheel. It put both binnacle lights out and washed away everything moveable. Braced in on port a little.

Sat 26th June 42 days out.
We had the forenoon watch and took in the fore upper topsail; the port watch took in the main lower topgallant. Carried coal for the galley and bogies plus general deck maintenance. Port watch set the mizzen lower topsail in the afternoon. In the 2nd dog watch both watches took in the mizzen upper topsail. The port outer buntline pin snapped which gave us a hard job including being washed into the scuppers by the big seas coming aboard and about drowned. Have had no sights for 3 days. The barometer has dropped although it is not blowing. We are all waiting for the blow. The captain managed to get a fix on a star tonight and we hope mark our position.

Sun 27th June 43 days out. Pos 93 degrees Lon W 52 degrees Lat S. Course ENE.
As the expected blow arrived we braced by the wind on the starboard tack. It laid us lee bulwarks under, and going about 12 knots. Between 6 and 7 we restowed sails that were breaking loose. Sails and rigging were caked thickly all over with ice. At 8 bells all hands were required to furl the main upper topsail. However it split at the starboard leech before we could smother it.

Foremast staysail blew out during the morning watch. Port watch rigged up a smothering centre extra buntline on the foresail. Did nothing in our afternoon except stand by under the forecastle head. Clear sky with frequent squalls the rest of the day.

Mon 28th June 44 days out. Course ESE.
Wind has hauled round to the SSW. During our morning watch we goose-winged the main lower topsail to repair the foot which had come adrift from the bolt rope. Most were engaged in repairing it. Cleared all the mess of swollen lines up and recoiled them. Port watch finished the running repairs and we all set it at the change of watch, also the foremast staysail and mizzen staysail. I managed to get an all-round wash this afternoon. It was freezing. Took the effort as it could be the last chance before the other side of the Horn.

Tues 29th June 45 days out.
During our afternoon watch we cut down the torn inner jib. I put new rovings on the foremast staysail and hauled down the mizzen staysail. The break chock somehow jumped out of a brace winch last night and it unwound till it was on the end seizing. The second mate said if we had not seen it in time and rewound it we could have been dismasted. About 3pm a big squall came up with snow and dark skies all around. Had 4 men at the wheel to put the helm over. On occasions she listed to 45 degrees. The squall slackened off around 11pm. I was wondering how much longer the foresail would have held. Our forecastle is hell to live in, water washing everywhere, smoke from the galley fire plus wet bunks, and men have to sleep here. Our course is ESE and we are trying to make as much southing as we can. We are only about 400 miles off the South American coast. The captain took no sights again today but with DR [dead reckoning] we should be 54d 3.7m S Lat and 86d 12.8m W Lon.

Wed 30th June. Lat 55d 57m S Lon 81d 45m W. Course E. Wind WSW.
Braced up nearly square. Cleared up the after deck again and many of us got our only re dried clothes wet again doing so. Mike braved snow squalls in temperatures below zero to mend the tear in the main upper topsail. Carried coal and firewood again to relight our bogie stoves. One man at the wheel again and only approx. 380 miles from the cape.

Thurs 1st July 47 days out. Pos Lat 56d 41.5m S Lon 77d. 25.6m W. Course E.
Squared up and running free. Had the afternoon watch. Set the fore and main upper topsails and the main lower topgallant. Snowed again today. Otherwise fine and sunny. Wind changed again tonight, so braced around on the starboard tack.

Friday 2nd July 48 days out.
Pos Lat 57d 13.1m S Lon 73d 26.8m W. Course ENE.
Squared up again last night in middle watch. Wind increased and we took in the main lower topgallant. Running heavily with two men at the wheel. It blew up more this morning and we hauled the sheet of the foresail forward. Both watches were called out and took in the fore and main upper topsails. I was sent from the wheel for not steering correctly. I got the blame for an argument between the second mate and the master which turned into a mad panic. Heavy snow squalls. Not far from the Horn now.

Sat 3rd July 49 days out. Pos Lat 57d 26m S Lon 67d 11m W.
Course NNE 3/4 E. Wind SW. 30mls off Staten Island and running free. The
other watch set the main upper topsail last night. Pip Small was up to loosen it
and could hardly get down as he was so frozen with cold, so we were told. I
set the upper topsail and Tom the main lower topgallant at 6 this morning in
our watch, it was still snowing and bloody cold. The port watch later set the
main upper topgallant. In the afternoon watch we set the mizzen upper topsail
and cleaned our forecastle out as best we could. Also set the foremast staysail.
The sea has moderated and the wind decreased. Passed Cape Horn's longitude
in the forenoon.

Sun 4th July 50 days out. Pos Lat 56d 22m S Lon 63d 45.5m W. Course NNE ¾E.
Wind strong, logging 5½ knots. Tom loosed fore upper topgallant. Port watch
set all staysails and we set the mainsail at noon when we came on watch. Set
all the topgallants. Sighted Cape Spaniard, Tierra Del Fuego, on the port beam
from up aloft and Staten Island ahead. The Master wants to make landfall off
the Falkland Islands. We are now making too much leeway, so both watches
took in the mainsail. Then we took in the fore upper topsail and the port watch
the mizzen one. We also took in the spanker. I tore my oilskins badly today.

Mon 5th July 51 days out. Pos Lat 55d 37.5m S Lon 62d 3m W. Course NNE ¾E.
Wind hauled round to the south and came on strong. Have logged 8½ knots
since noon. Later after setting more sail we were doing up to 11½ knots with
the wind on the quarter. The seas are running high, plenty of water on deck.
Took in main and mizzen staysails. At the first dog watch both watches took
in the mizzen upper topsail. Are passing over a sand bank. Heaving the hand
lead every 2 hours.
Whilst at the wheel this afternoon, the steering wire parted as if cut with a
chisel and she started to come up into the wind. I told the 2nd mate and he
dashed aft to engage the auxiliary wheel. So I had to give the 2 whistles for
our watch to come aft and help. Four of us put the after wheel over and we
were soon back on our old course without any mishap. In certain circumstances
we could have come aback and in heavy weather be dismasted. There is now
¾ of a point difference on the compass aft. One on the wheel again.

Tues 6th July 52 days out. No position. Course NNE ¾E.
This morning we set all topgallants. At last we are cracking on some sail.
Took out the midship steering wire. The port watch seized and cut a new one
from the coil. In the dog watch we took in all the upper topgallants so that
effort did not last long. We are all used to steering from aft now. This was
where all older type sailing vessels' steering wheels were situated.
We are very near the Falklands now and will pass to the east of them. Last
night we passed over the north bank. Whilst sounding with the deep lead line
we lost the lead so used a belaying pin instead.

*

So at last we were round Cape 'Stiff' on our last lap home. Everyone's spirits
were high. We could now look forward to the tropics ahead, to dry bunks and
clothes, to sleeping on deck and of course making a quick passage up the
Atlantic and dropping the hook in Falmouth harbour.

Chapter 10

THE LONG HAUL NORTH

After making landfall off the Falkland Islands where we readjusted our navigation errors by soundings, bearings and time corrections, we beat north very slowly as preservation of our sails still had priority over taking advantage of fair and favourable winds. After taking 49 days to the Horn we were to take another 49 days to the Line owing to the continual and unnecessary reduction of sail which was ordered whenever we had a chance of making extra knots and a good day's run. However the old adage prevailed: 'Ours is not to question why, ours is but to do and die'.

The hope we had when departing Port Victoria of a reasonable run of 100 days was well dashed and we resigned ourselves to a long hard haul up the south and north Atlantic in a monotonous round of undersailing. The master's and the owner's view obviously was that if there was no extra profit to be made by an early delivery of our cargo then the savings that could be achieved on our meagre wages and sustenance by shortening our time at sea were negligible compared to the possible expense of the loss of canvas or of other repair. Our desire for a smart passage home did not come into the equation.

In the last days of the sailing ship trade the newspapers used to make headlines each year with the so-called 'grain races'. It appealed to the romantic readers keen on adventure stories, but was to a large extent a modern legend created by journalists. If there had been racing between the tea clippers in the days when there was a big monetary advantage to being able to auction the season's first chests of tea at the markets, this urgency did not apply to the same degree to the grain trade. And as it was very rare for two contemporary vessels to depart on the same day from the same port or even from any other Gulf port, the conditions for a real race did not exist.

Gradually the weather and temperature improved and the snow and sleet squalls diminished to mere rain-filled blasts. We took down the coils of all the lines that had been hung up on hooks, on backstays or on the lifelines to prevent them being washed over the side, and recoiled them on their respective pins on the rails. Then down came the lifelines and the nets above the gunwales. Frayed or damaged cordage was systematically repaired or replaced. Any other repairs necessary aloft were dealt with after initial inspection by the topman, then by a mate if it was a bigger job that needed more hands or new gear meaning expense for the owner.

About the latitude of the River Plate we resumed Swedish watches and with this transition started the preparation for painting every piece of metal inboard around every deck. This was the custom of all ships homeward bound. They had to arrive back in Europe looking spick and span so the owners could see first hand that their investment was being maintained properly and that their crews had been 'gainfully employed'. A vessel's appearance outboard was ignored as everyone knew that it was impossible to look like a new steamboat out of a picture book after a long voyage through weather that would strip paint off anything, but masts and spars were expected to have been recently coated and touched up whilst in the fair-weather trade-wind period.

At last we were able to open the top half of the steel door that was our entrance onto the foredeck. But it was still winter in the south Atlantic and the green seas were prone to roar over the bulwarks filling the foredeck.

The new hands had acclimatised to the conditions on board and survived well. Except for one youngster of our age, they were all older, a couple being over 40. Most of the Australians had signed on for the voyage to the UK and were not professional seamen, except young Peters who later did a second round trip, the final voyage of the *Passat* under the Finnish flag. Peters eventually took his second mate's certificate and stayed at sea.

Of the Finns only a few were now left from the original crew. They were now the leading hands except for the sailmaker's job held competently by Mike Ruffhead. Our former carpenter Franz Forsman who had been promoted to acting third mate in the mates' watch, after experiencing this elevated position up the command ladder for a while became unhappy with his new lot and decided it was not his forte. I am of the opinion that he had personal differences with the mate, now his immediate superior. He asked the master for his old job back and after negotiation he returned to his trade.

The master chose Ingvar Sundquist, who had taken on the carpenter's duties as he was apt in handling the tools of this trade, to now become acting third mate. Ingvar performed this task very well and with fair authority until he signed off with the rest of us in Avonmouth. This promotion was invaluable for his future. Paying off with a discharge stating he had been an acting watchkeeping mate was a fine recommendation for one so young in that era of shipping. He later went on to obtain his second mate's ticket with sail endorsement and finally became the Commodore Master of one of Finland's shipping lines.

The master held the other watch with our former donkeyman, Marti Suomi, now acting second mate. However after observing the latter's competency he often went below after the watch handover was complete leaving his new acting mate in charge, but with orders to be called for any sail handling or navigational changes. In very bad conditions or at any critical times he would rest, or sleep if possible, on the chartroom settee.

As we edged north and the weather and temperature improved we were able to bail out our forecastle, then, after scrubbing it, to air it and dry it out. On the first Sunday we could take advantage of (with regard to having free time without being called out to help the other watch) we braved the cold and with buckets of water heated on the galley stove, courtesy of the cook, scrubbed ourselves all over in the washhouse forward. Those who had sheets and pillowcases washed them also and hung them to dry under the forecastle head. It was marvellous to feel clean linen and clean underclothes on one's body again.

We were all hygiene-conscious: we had been taught well by the Finns who are a very fastidious people as to cleanliness. Our living conditions made standards hard to maintain as we were cramped in tiny quarters with only a half-bucket ration of cold water per day for ablutions. Hot water was seldom available, and the washrooms were forward and unreachable sometimes for days in heavy weather. But on the whole we did our best.

Our first water tank was now empty and a couple of men from each watch were detailed to scale its inside. After red-leading the scaled areas the whole tank was painted and when dry was again coated with a lime wash. It was now ready for filling with sweet fresh rain water when we reached the latitudes of tropical rain squalls and we had an even keel to hold the water on deck long enough to fill the tanks. This opportunity presented itself early. When we were 60 days out the strong winds petered out and we wore ship round onto the port tack, which left us on an unusually steady and even keel. Heavy rain descended from the heavens for the next twenty-four hours. We hastened to take advantage of this gift, blocked all the freeing ports and scuppers. Our empty tank was soon filled and the second one topped up. As we were becalmed, and even though it was still cold, most took the opportunity to have a dhobi-fest on the foredeck and washed any still unwashed garments, and some of us also washed our blankets or at least one of our two.

Of course all this surplus fresh water also gave the mate the opportunity of working the watches round the clock at holystoning the high decks while the rain lasted with no wind to interrupt the task. Eventually, before we were ordered onto the well decks, away came the wind, and after trimming yards and braces, then reducing sails, we were back at our usual routine.

After a few uneventful days of undersailing and painting we were all employed on reeving off the new steering wires for the midship wheel. These stretched from midship on either side through lead blocks, then down onto the after well deck and into the poop at deck level through the bulkhead, and so right aft to the rudder quadrant situated in the after lazaret. These new wires had been spliced, cut and readied by our ABs Bill Hillwood and Hans Hongel.

This proved a longer task than one would imagine. The wire had to be an exact length and to make the required number of turns on the wheel drum so as to take the quadrant from its fore-and-aft position to hard over on either side. When one side of the wire was pulling, the other side had to slack by exactly the same amount. To complicate matters, for the greater length of its run along the decks the wire was under a metal protective cover. We pulled it through this obstacle with the aid of a light line that we had taken the precaution of marrying to the broken end of the old wire before taken it out.

We had become quite used to steering from aft on the poop, so to us there was no great hurry to complete the job. The danger of steering from this position had disappeared now that we were well up into the Atlantic and therefore free of the poop-threatening 'greybeards' of the southern oceans.

At about this time we assessed our losses on the voyage so far. With sail and rigging we had suffered minimal damage which was soon rectified and repaired. Lost sails were replaced and new ones prescribed to be made when we had no further replacements in the locker. Our personal losses were not considerable either: some clothing ripped and torn and headwear blown off and lost. Most crockery used for meals had been smashed; this upset the saloon but we were not affected as we used tin utensils.

During the heavy-rain period the master had become very wary and agitated, fearing the encounter of pamperos and so had us reduce sail to storm canvas. However as we traversed the area prone to such disturbances all we experienced were two occasions of intense lightning following a rapid fall of the barometer. At times we watched the incredible ghostly St Elmo's fire travelling along the bare yards and up and down the masts. Thankfully there was no follow-up with violent winds and eventually this atmospheric phenomenon was left behind.

Our master, of course, had every reason to be apprehensive and to take precautions knowing that many vessels have been caught unprepared and severely damaged, even dismasted and sunk, in these latitudes. With a mostly unproven crew, the majority of his present complement making their first trip deep sea, he was right to steer on the side of caution.

The next day we picked up a steady wind and proceeded to tack our way as close as possible to a northerly course. This day was also the day of reckoning for the last of the pigs which was this time dispatched humanely with a bullet from the master's revolver. That evening we dined on the usual blood pudding and berry sauce. And for the next couple of days it was the proverbial pork stew or rather soup with bits of fatty pork in it. The fresh meat dishes, however they were cooked, were a welcome change from the tinned food which was the basis of the menu during this homeward voyage.

The wind had strengthened and the cross seas kept the well decks full of water preventing any further painting on these, so we continued to pretty up the high decks, the poop, midship and forecastle head. We knocked down the pig pens and painted under the head. Soon the wind reached gale force and we were back to storm canvas with two men at the wheel.

An excerpt from my log describes the scenario.

Tues 20th July 66 days out. Pos Lat 35d 3m S Lon 33d 16m W.
By the wind. Course E/N.
Logging 8 knots. Scraping teak rails on the flying bridge in our morning watch. This evening the wind reached gale force. Took in main upper topgallant. Tried to take in the outer jib but it blew out before we could accomplish the exercise. The mizzen staysail also blew out. Took in inner jib and jigger staysail. The mate called out the free watch and we all took in the three lower topgallants. I helped with the fore and main. We are now shortened down again to storm canvas.
In our middle free watch we were called out only 20 min after we had turned in. This was to take in the three upper topsails. The mizzen came in first, then as we were coming down to the deck the port sheet of the fore upper topsail parted. All hands went to the bunt and clew lines but before we could clew it up it had blown to pieces and the flying loose chain sheet had ripped a great hole in the lower topsail. This then split from head to foot with a crash like thunder. Then came an extra blow with blinding rain and we were ordered to leave that sail and to save the main upper topsail before it also blew out. However it came in handsomely after a titanic battle by both watches who got it furled and lashed with extra gaskets. Then back down we came and into the swimming pool of a foredeck where we once again manned the pin-rails to clew up the remains of the fore upper topsail and up again to furl the tattered pieces and down once more presuming we were finished. Alas we were ordered to goose-wing the mizzen lower topsail but in the end we furled the whole sail. By this time we had been on deck mainly aloft for 13 hours straight and were now again on watch.

Wed 21st July 67 days out. Wind S hard. Course NE/N.
Pos Lat 34d 30m S Lon 30d 50m W.
In the forenoon the port watch sent down the lower fore topsail and got out another from the sail locker. In our afternoon watch and with the help of the port watch we bent the new lower fore topsail. Our watch then hauled out again from the locker a new flying jib. The wind dropped this evening and the

port watch was able to square up the decks a bit and then they set the main upper topsail. Then we followed in our watch setting the main lower topgallant.

Thurs 22nd July 68 days out. Course NE.
In our morning watch we hauled out and repaired another upper topsail. Then in the afternoon we were called out to help the port watch to bend this topsail. This morning we also had set the mizzen upper topsail getting soaked through in the process. The port watch set the mizzen lower topgallant and managed to stay dry. We are now braced square and running free. It has turned out a warm and lovely day and we are wearing only pants and shirt. However we are now rolling badly with the wind right aft but the seas crossing.
The course was changed at noon. It is my 18th birthday today. Before the watch ended we set the main upper topgallant. It seems the bad blow has passed over and we are clapping on sail again. We are all hoping there will be no more casualties with our sails.

*

Within a few days the gale moderated, the clouds disappeared and the sun began to thaw us out. We noticed about this time that we had lost our constant companions of the southern oceans, the albatrosses. This told us we were well up into the Atlantic as these great birds seldom venture north of the Tropic of Capricorn. But the storm had been another blow to our hope of making a respectable passage and of soon experiencing the long-awaited tropics.
We had expected to pick up the SE trade winds by now but again we were disappointed. The sailor's oft saying of 'more days more dollars' held no respect from any of us for none earned enough per day to compensate for the drudgery we were experiencing on this never-ending voyage.
Adding to our plight since rounding the Horn was the unusual amount of days we spent rolling in cross-sea swells. Except when becalmed, especially in the doldrums latitudes, sailing ships seldom rolled even when running free with the wind right aft, as the wind pressure in even a shortened-down spread of sails should, in normal circumstances, keep a vessel on a fairly even keel. But now we were not spreading enough canvas to counter the huge swell which consequently rolled us unmercifully. We were literally 'rolling home'! Such conditions put a massive weight strain on the tophamper which was for long periods flying through the air in a huge arch one way, then the other, with a sickening jolt at the change of direction.
This made working aloft especially tricky as one continuously needed to find means of hanging on and steadying oneself when trying to use both hands to perform any task. When off watch and trying to sleep, it meant wedging yourself into your bunk to avoid being thrown out. The old Navy hammock would have been ideal in these conditions but we would not have had the space in our forecastles to swing them.

*

My experience at sea and in sail, all twenty months or more of it, had been moulding both my character and physique. Although still with some time to continue growing, I was no longer so skinny and had developed hard muscles in all limbs. This was a good result as only eighteen months before going to sea I had sustained near fatal accidental injuries which could have impeded my development and prevented me even from going to sea. My mother had been very worried when I left for Finland, wondering whether I had recovered enough for the physical challenge posed on a square-rigged sailing ship.

The accident happened whilst riding a delivery bike carrying meat orders from the butcher I was working for at the time. When riding on a busy street I had been distracted by an aeroplane passing over low just above the rooftops. I looked up at it and in doing so wandered over the dividing line into oncoming traffic and hit the bonnet grille of a milk float lorry. I was in hospital for over six months having sustained two fractures of the skull, a broken collarbone and lacerations.

The serious damage was to the top vertebra, the atlas bone. This was split in half by constriction from the force of my head being thrust downwards at impact. In other words I had a broken neck. However, being young and full of vigour and confidence, I made a remarkable recovery. So successful was this recovery that within one year I passed the Shipping Federation medical at Dock Street pool, they being ignorant of my medical history and my mop of hair now covering the deep laceration scars on my skull. Over the following two years I had no real after-effects from this traumatic experience which did not seem to interfere with my physical growth, and so I was able to pull my weight with the best at my size at any sailorising job I was shown.

As for character, I cannot say that I had developed ultimate wisdom, but I had at least grown used to living in harmony with those around me, mindful of not doing anything that would upset others' lives. When ten individuals exist in such a small space as our forecastle each becomes very considerate of the others. Before making any move or noise you reflect whether you yourself would object to anyone else doing the same. Such caution sometimes suppresses the exuberance of youthful lads but it is necessary for survival under these extreme conditions. And it is certainly a good lesson for life.

On the other hand, I confess that I had also picked up unhealthy attitudes to life to complement the role model I had chosen for myself. Most of these were luckily dispensed with as I grew older.

At that age I was anxious to be 'one of the boys' and to impress others. I was also too easily influenced and believed as gospel most of what I was told. So I tried to appear tough, unmoved and unbending, without any compassion.

Romance did not exist for me for many years after the break-off with the girl I had left behind in England and the unfortunate Malayan experience. I put these memories out of mind and pretended that love was all lies and sentimental nonsense, unworthy of hard men. Although I am sure I would have been very happy to have someone to care deeply for me, most later encounters with women for me were devoid of true feelings as I was never ashore long enough to develop a natural association with any.

My experience of womanly delights came, with one or two exceptions, from 'good-time girls' or from prostitutes, mainly those that worked in brothels, and I approached the whole question from a rather cynical viewpoint.

I saw it as a gamble as far as costs were concerned. For with the good-time girls one could spend a fair amount of one's sub on the drink and entertainment expected by these ladies before they 'succumbed' to a sailor's desires. This choice also meant that by the time the necessary preliminaries were accepted and bed or bunk was at last made the sailor was often too 'full' to perform. Sometimes both parties were in such condition.

So I found that the best method of satisfaction was to go straight to the brothel with all one's faculties intact, whereby one obtained his money's worth. It was never sensible to make this choice after getting inebriated, as many did, for if you did not perform in the given time limit you either paid again or, if you could not afford to, you were shown out and left a very frustrated man.

Another reason to prefer the professionals was that they always check their clients diligently for signs of gonorrhoea or syphilis before allowing any contact. And the girls working in brothels generally have regular medical checks for venereal disease for their own sake and for the business's reputation.

With good-time girls you could never be sure they had not become infected, even though most are usually careful in the choice of their partners and often take the precaution of periodic checks for VD. Some irresponsible sick-minded fools unfortunately pass on their disease in full knowledge of their predicament.

Such was the introduction to sex and woman that I had obtained since leaving home and going to sea. Not especially edifying, but I presumed from then on that this was the normal attitude expected of a smart sailor and I was quite pleased with myself.

*

Our main work now when on daylight watch, apart from sailing necessities, was soogying, chipping and scraping, then undercoating the deck fittings, hatch coamings, bulkheads and bulwarks. The bulkheads and bulwarks were then to be painted white with black borders, the coamings, deck fittings and machinery black and grey, the brace winches and other small items of rigging bottle green.

As usual, the port and starboard watches performed their various tasks from their respective sides to the centre of the deck.

The work was often interrupted by rain, seas and spray. In inclement weather we were put onto scraping and varnishing the teak woodwork: pin and fife rails, wheel box, chartroom, etc. The sail repair gang was also increased at this time as much repair was to be done to the heavy-weather sails that had to be replaced, while our fine-weather canvas also had to be made ready.

One unusual and interesting job which broke the monotony of paint work was to shift the broken lifeboat from the *Viking* which was being returned to Mariehamn. It had been lifted aboard before we sailed and lashed on the after deck. As it had continually obstructed several sailing jobs it was decided to shift it forward to the starboard side of the foredeck.

This was done by rigging a gin block on the after side of the mainmast crosstree cheeks and reeving a gantline, the end of which was made fast to the lifting strops around the boat. The gantline was then taken to a deck capstan by which means the boat was lifted while being guided on its way forward and up onto the midship deck. On achieving this first move the boat was temporarily rested on this deck whilst Martin and I re-rigged the block and gantline in the similar position abaft the foremast. The port watch then took over and again lifted the boat, guiding it forward onto the foredeck and eventually lowering it and relashing it in its new position where it was less of an obstruction for the rest of the voyage. Whether this boat ever ended up back in Mariehamn I have no idea; all I remember is that it was slung ashore by crane in Avonmouth and disappeared up the wharf.

During this period of our effort to head north we were often becalmed, which gave us opportunity, now the weather had improved, to have a try at shark catching. As we had already found when outward bound, Atlantic sharks are very fussy. But we caught a few and were able to observe the professional method of dispatching and cutting up these denizens of the deep. This exercise was carried out by one of our new hands, Corigliano, who had been a professional trawler fisherman. Corrie, as he was nicknamed, was from Beechport in South Australia and was of Italian immigrant descent.

Another pastime I indulged in whilst we drifted, with Tom and Bob, two other new hands, was diving and swimming over the side. This we found extremely exhilarating but we did not stay in long as the water was still cold and we were well aware that sharks could be lying in hiding under our hull waiting for a chance to turn the tables on us and have a meal of fresh meat.

The boredom of going nowhere for days, or often drifting in the wrong direction, of wallowing and continuously rolling in a cross swell, eventually got to a few of the new hands, mainly those in the port watch. On two occasions, when off watch, they decided to dispel the monotony by opening their personal cache of grog, in this case the rum they had surreptitiously brought with them. Most of the hands in that watch were around 25–35 years. They were not the easily disciplined young fellows we had been with the former mates and our elders, and they tended to take advantage of the weakening of command caused by the shortage of senior officers on this trip.

Of the eight men that took part in these session six became incapable of standing their watch. Hangovers were very apparent on the following watches and one fellow was out cold for seventeen hours. It was sheer good fortune that during this time there were no navigational changes or manoeuvres. If we had had to tack or wear ship, or even to reduce or make any sail, accidents would have occurred, I am sure. Once the demon drink was consumed common sense prevailed again and discipline rectified itself.

Many whales were around the vessel at this time, moving back south for the brief Antarctic summer. We knew that their number would be depleted very soon by the hungry whaling fleets that were waiting to intercept them. They seemed to know we posed no danger to them, perhaps because we had no engine, and they came very close, some nearly alongside. They had apparently lost the memory of the old wind-driven whalers, which had now been superseded for over 60 years by the modern fleets that can harvest these wonderful animals by the hundreds.

Drifting, tacking north when blessed with favourable winds, we at last crossed the Tropic of Capricorn. However at this time of the year the summer was in the northern hemisphere and we did not enjoy the long-expected tropical weather until we worked further north towards the equator.

The SE trades were still elusive, but finally, as we were 90 days out, we received the full benefit of those wonderful winds that pushed us northwards at 5–6 knots or more.

Our painting endeavour was interrupted over the next few days as we changed our sails for a fair-weather set. At this point a couple more men were put into Mike's sail gang along with Ingvar, our third mate, to make up the six needed.

A few of the new hands around this time also became sick, mainly in the port watch. They were laid up and excused from duty on a day-to-day basis after inspection by the master. Bob Deacon, who had become lamp trimmer, also went down with a high temperature and erupted in a rash, so the master isolated him to a cabin under the poop. I took over his lamp duties while he was incapacitated as I had done the job before.

These casualties meant extra work for those left fit. It also resulted in the watch going below often being held on deck to complete a job together with the short-handed relief who could not complete it on their own. The watch below was also more likely to be pulled out to assist the short watch in a job now beyond them. So although there was genuine sympathy for anyone struck with a sickness it was given with the hope of a miraculous recovery.

We crossed the line in the evening of Sunday 22nd August, 99 days out. Although a few of the new hands had never crossed the line before there was no thought of any ceremony under the circumstances.

The steering wires had to be shortened owing to stretching and it was back to the wheel on the poop whilst that task was in progress. This did not affect the helmsman at all but it meant that the mate of the watch had to go forward to the midship chartroom if he wanted to consult the chart.

The trades were holding firm and we were bowling along day after day averaging around six knots. This was phenomenal as these trades often peter out before the equator where one usually encounters a belt of doldrums with hardly a breath of wind. This year it seemed possible that we might even pass from the SE trades to the NE trades without being caught in this windless zone to wallow helplessly.

We now had schools of porpoises playing around our bows and their sight cheered us up. Marti Suomi predicted 30 days to Falmouth. We fixed a stern light aft to conform with the Rules of the Road now that we were nearing the steamer routes. This lamp I had happily primed and given an extra polish before affixing it.

Sure enough, when 104 days out, along came the SS *Debrett* of the Lamport and Holt Company proceeding from Manchester to Rio. We spoke to her as she circled us. She assured us that she would report us to Lloyds, the shipping insurance company.

This period of the voyage was a wonderful time. We were able to take great advantage of the warm tropical temperature cooled by a steady strong breeze. With the wind on the quarter and all sails drawing well the vessel lay over on a steady comfortable angle. And it felt so good to climb and work aloft without being encumbered with heavy clothes and oilskins! We only wore shorts in daytime now and were soon well suntanned once again.

In such ideal conditions, one forgets the hard times and thoroughly enjoys what is good and beautiful about a sailing vessel. When high up aloft overhauling buntlines or engaged in a maintenance job, one is able to pause a while and take in the grand atmosphere of the open ocean. All you can hear around you is the rigging that creaks and sings under the strain of the steady wind pressure and you feel as in a world of your own.

The vista from out on the end of an upper yardarm is exhilarating: the horizon stretching to infinity wherever you look, the blue sky with a few white clouds meeting a dark blue-green sea. Then you look down and watch the vessel below, pencil like, knifing through the short chop of the waves. Streaming behind, the white wake gives you a feeling of easy speed, though you probably do not make much more than eight knots. Oh, if only it was always like this! You soak it all up while you can.

This was the chance to get out of our cramped forecastle when watch below, at night especially. Some slept in the safety net either side of the jib-boom, others on No. 2 hatch, whilst those who had made hammocks slung them in positions out of the way of the watch tending sails.

This idyllic period however came to an end with the disappearance of the SE trades around 7–8 degrees north. We had hoped they would continue further north than this. Within a few days some wind came away from the west and with it heavy rain giving us another opportunity to replenish our water tanks and to wash our clothes during our free watch.

These conditions prevailed as we manoeuvred north till around 13 degrees north and it was in the vicinity of the Cape Verde Islands that we caught the NE trades on 30th August, 107 days out. As they came away we wore ship to go on the other tack.

The NE trades in this area were at times quite strong with a few squalls. On one occasion the wind kept changing right around the compass. We reckoned we were passing through a hurricane zone. All hands were called to reduce sail and to attend braces as we 'boxed the compass' to keep up with the revolving wind.

We were all fatigued from the long and heavy work involved over that period of continual bracing, so it was decided to put all the watch keepers that had been temporary day workers back into the watches so as to ease the workload. The lamp trimmer's job I had taken over I passed on to Martin who had it till he paid off.

For the next few days we had excellent sailing weather and averaged 7–8 knots. The trades seemed to be coming more from the east than the north-east. Consequently, unusual as it was, we were able to steer a NNE course, the direction we actually wished to proceed on.

Mike and his diminished sail gang were steadily working on the massive new foresail using 00 canvas (storm gauge) during this period. This was a huge job and they did well at this task. Mike had lost his special palm repairing a royal while still bent. He cut out another from heavy leather and pig skin which sufficed well for the job.

Our master was pleased to see all this productive work proceeding and he appeared relaxed, probably reflecting on the fact that the worst part of his command was nearly over and that he could now look forward to a safe arrival in the near future. He had a fit of generosity and he cut out enough from a bolt of No. 2 canvas for Martin and myself to make sea bags from.

One of the tedious jobs we started now, after we had finished painting everything we could on all decks within the bulwarks, was scraping all the paint spots off the teak decking in preparation for oiling it. The two junior mates started varnishing the already prepared and oiled chartroom, binnacles, wheel box, wheels, skylight lids, pin and fife rails and all other teak fittings.

All this conjured up hopes and expectations, and the main topic of conversation at this time, especially between the remaining members of the original crew, was what each of us was going to do when we arrived home, although we always abstained to disclose our most intimate hopes to our shipmates.

Quite a few ships were sighted, some of which altered course to come and inspect this apparition from a bygone era. Some even tried to engage us by signalling. However our competence at signal communication was terrible.

The new foresail was completed at last. It would be stretched and bent as soon as we were out of the tropics and into the north Atlantic, where we hoped to pick up the westerlies. Mike and Eric Mann his main assistant now turned their attention to cutting out and sewing up a new spanker sail. For this they used the bolt rope from an old 1928 spanker. The cordage was in excellent condition and it was predicted that it would last longer than our new coils of boltrope.

When we reached the edge of the Sargasso Sea our favourable wind died out and left us wallowing in large expanses of weed drifting with the current. A few of us took advantage of us being becalmed and as it was still warm we chanced swimming over the side, often encountering patches of weed teeming with marine life. For over two days we drifted with the current. As there were plenty of rain squalls we continued to top up our water tanks by blocking scuppers and freeing ports at every opportunity.

Instead of carrying on with our fair-weather sails to take maximum advantage of the faint breezes we now received the 'old man' had us change to storm canvas. This we presumed was in anticipation of strong westerlies suddenly being encountered without the time to safely make the sail change. This proved another waste of time and wind for it was another couple of days before we received the westerlies and when they arrived they were weak.

So the order was given to make all sail again. The master's caution over carrying too much sail was illustrated again two days later. We were at last bowling along at a fair speed for us, when a vessel, the C L Celo passed astern of us and signalled 'Where are you bound?' Our master immediately ordered the reduction of sail, so in came the royals and upper topgallants. We heard later via the galley 'information service' that he read the message as 'Weather deteriorating, blow imminent.' It happened that there was a rain squall overhead at the time, which must have contributed to his misinterpreting the signal.

The standard of signalling on the Passat was appalling. None of the mates could attempt the exercise as the second was the former donkeyman and the third was Ingvar Sundquist who had not had pre-sea training. However Ingvar was the only one of the afterguard not to panic on the occasions when vessels tried to talk to us. The only more or less knowledgeable persons on these matters were Martin, Terry and Bob Deacon, and in this instance the master did not consult any of them.

We carried no means for visual Morse signalling except a battery torch. But anyway no one had any competence at Morse either, except these lads again.

As we entered further into the shipping lanes we encountered increasing traffic and several vessels tried to communicate with us, but there was no point in attempting any intercourse unless the lads were called out to help. This happened when the British tanker Lapanus passed astern of us. This time it was in the starboard watch's period so Martin and Bob, with me assisting, took control of the signalling after getting the nod from the master via the mate. Bob manned the halyard, I the downhaul and Martin read the other vessel's hoists and readied the flags needed for the answer. This time there was no mistake. 'Are you fitted with radio?' Answer 'No.' 'Do you wish your position to be reported?' Answer 'No.' 'Bon voyage from Lapanus.' Answer from us 'Thank you from Passat and bon voyage to you.' Even then the captain and the mate started arguing between themselves and tried to interfere.

Several more attempts were made at speaking to ships of many nationalities, even to a Shaw Saville passenger ship one evening. The best communication came when 140 days out and nearing landfall. We had passed through a fleet of French fishing trawlers when the wind fell right away leaving us becalmed once more. A cargo ship passed astern then another cargo vessel hove in sight and came right up nearly alongside. It proved to be the *Sea Queen* of Panamanian registry. Many foreign shipping companies or owners put their vessels under this flag of convenience as a means of making bigger profits, as this nation required few regulations for safety or insurance. This was also a way of avoiding paying tax on profit. In this case the owners were most possibly Norwegian.

As this vessel slowed right down her captain hailed us and asked for our captain by name through a speaking trumpet. They were so close that a heaving line could have been placed on her deck. Their captain was Christian Backman from the Åland Islands. The two had a brief conversation. Then the melodious Finnish language sang out across the short stretch of water. It was none other than the first Finn to jump ship, Vilowa Luouta. And two more Finns that we knew joined in asking after several who had left us. Vilowa told Ingvar Sundquist that he was earning the big dollars where he was and was happy he had made the move.

The next day two more notable exchanges took place. One was with a Victory ship the *Sylvia Lykes* from New York. The Lykes Line was quite a large east-coast company. She tried to speak to us by Aldis lamp but it was useless. Then along came a fast banana boat heading for London from Kingston, Jamaica. She was the *Jamaica Producer*. She flew a hoist WAY meaning 'bon voyage'. We just managed to get back OVF or 'thank you' before she was too far off to for any further conversation.

Chapter 11

COMING HOME

The temperature had now cooled considerably as we sailed NE up the Atlantic in the westerlies. We had made the full change of sails to the heavy set, bending our brand new foresail that fitted perfectly, and sent down the by now rather threadbare set for repair and stowage. Out came all our winter gear from our lockers and we got to the task of recoating our oilskins.

Quite a few were now sewing up sea bags. Mine was nearly finished. I completed it with a bottom handle spliced into the treble-layered bottom by way of star grommet holes.

I then applied myself to the handles of my new sea chest which had been handsomely made by Franz Forsman, our chippy. It was constructed of tough but light timber with the four sides sloping inwards from the bottom up, a flat top and the usual double bottom. The handles I made around a six-strand extra flexible one-inch steel wire rope as the core. An eye splice was fashioned in each end so that the bolt would pass through these two eyes when the wire was bent into the shape of a horse-shoe type handle. This wire was packed to make it thicker in the middle where it fitted into the hand, then parcelled and finally cross-pointed with strips of black and red leather. The old type of chest handle was made completely of rope except for the metal bar, but our new method I am sure was infinitely superior.

Sea chests were in use in the latter days of sail when seamen took away with them their few possessions on voyages. The days were then past when men shipped with only the clothes they stood in, although that still happened right up to the war of 1914 when shanghaiing finally disappeared. Men after that period took away warm clothes, boots, oilskins, toilet gear, tools of trade and personal things, even books, all stowed in their sea chests. When at sea a man's go-ashores were stored there too. The chest was used to sit on in the forecastle. Its double bottom was to prevent the sea water which perpetually lapped the deck of the forecastle in heavy weather from eventually seeping into the chest and ruining the contents.

As accommodation improved on sailing vessels the usefulness of a sea chest diminished. The watches were moved from under the old forecastle head into deck houses and into the midship section of the three-island vessels, and mess tables and bench seats were installed, as well as lockers and even drawers for each man's gear. I really did not need a chest on the *Passat* and I was the only hand to ship with one.

However, after it was smashed to pieces on the voyage out, I kept lamenting its loss, and eventually Franz kindly promised to make me a new one in his spare time. The result was a spectacular creation, especially after I had attached the intricate new handles and painted the outside a deep indigo blue. The inside I painted white, and Adrian Small painted a beautiful picture of *Passat* under full sail inside the lid.

So, having joined with what I considered a family treasure, I was now able to pay off with a fitting replacement which would in turn become a witness of my younger years at sea for posterity.

I may add that I did not take it to sea on any of my subsequent voyages, but it had many different uses ashore over the years. My mother sent it to me when I settled in Australia much later, on which occasion I had a humorous brush with an overzealous and stubborn customs officer who had measured the inside and outside depths of the chest and, on account of the double bottom, concluded that there was a secret compartment probably packed with prohibited imports!

*

Our passage now became a frustrating succession of stop-and-gos as the west wind continually rose then fell away. This was very detrimental to our morale as we edged closer to the coasts of France and home. A few feigned indifference whilst others openly cursed our bad fortune with the winds. I am sure all on board were praying for a better deal from the god of wind. One day would bring strong westerlies and a big sea so that we were able to run free on an easterly course passing vessels which went westward into heavy seas and disappeared into troughs. The next day would see us in a big swell with no wind and a sea mist swirling all around. When the swell was very bad we took in the high sails and brailed up the courses for the rolling put a huge strain on the rigging.

Meanwhile we were kept fully occupied preparing our floating home for arrival, while always standing by, ready to drop whatever we were working at and jump to sheeting home, setting sail and trimming yards if the wind returned to drive us again towards our destination.

On 30th September and 137 days out we were only some 200 miles off, and as we were slowly closing the distance to landfall the excitement, at least for us young ones who had never made a full voyage around the world, was mounting.

In this state of mind, we found our next work most enjoyable. It was to break out and rig our anchors for use on arrival. It took us a full day, each watch readying their own side's anchor, but it was a sailorising job eagerly performed now that we were homeward bound.

140 days out on 3rd October. After experiencing mist and intermittent breeze, a steady wind at last came away from the north, almost a headwind for us. We now had to weave our way between fishing trawlers that could not evade us owing to having their nets down, so all stood by for a collision which luckily never eventuated. But the presence of these trawlers forced us to reduce our speed. Then at midday we had to wear ship onto the other tack.

While I was up taking in royals and upper topgallants, I sighted land on the port beam which proved to be the Scilly Islands off Lands End. Blighty at last! What a wonderful feeling of anticipation it brought to me!

At eight the following morning, at change of watch, we wore ship again and set a course, allowed by the wind's direction, to pass clear of the Lizard headland before turning and heading for Falmouth. We set upper topgallants again to assist in countering the current which pushed us towards the shore.

The manoeuvre was unsuccessful. We were unable to clear the Lizard, and in the evening dogwatch, in the face of frustrating headwinds, we had to wear ship once more to make southing on a ESE course. At midnight we repeated our attempt and failed again.

My personal log entry for that day is a good illustration of the difficulty of working a square-rigged sailing vessel against contrary winds into a position from where it can further proceed safely on a new course towards its destination.

5th October 142 days out.
Tacked ship this morning at 8am. Heading NNE. Tacked again at 1pm. Heading SE. Wind went round and we are heading SSW so all hands wore ship at 4pm. Tacked ship again at 7pm. Just could not make it round the Lizard. Wind went round once more another point and a half, so we were called out again in our free watch at 10pm and tacked ship again. Heading NE+E. Lizard now on our port bow. May have a chance of clearing this headland now. Wind freshening, port watch took in the upper topgallants just before midnight. It is getting quite cold now.

This continuous conflict between the wind direction and the intended course of a vessel was part of sailing ship life. The English Channel was a frequent scene of such contest. In the clipper ship era many a crack passage outward bound was ruined by headwinds encountered from the start when casting off the tug, or down the Channel after clearing the Downs. Again when homeward bound after a marvellous run of fair wind all the way from the China coast, many a clipper hoping to set a new record was brought up hard against obstinate and persistent headwinds. It was not unusual for vessels to spend two or three weeks on those occasions beating either way to clear the channel.

At last we overcame the whimsical wind, cleared the headland and, 143 days out from Port Victoria, made the anchorage designated for ships awaiting orders, right opposite Falmouth castle.

For three days we lay at anchor, during which time we kept watches, as we could have been ordered at any time to proceed to our discharge port. On the second day the captain went ashore with the local agent and received our orders from Clarkson's, our company's agents in London. When he returned we learnt via the galley 'information office' that we were to discharge all our cargo at the port of Avonmouth situated on the starboard side of the Bristol Channel.

It was a fairly new port at the time. It had been built to accommodate the ever-growing size of the ocean-going vessels which could no longer reach safely the old port of Bristol up the Avon river. This passage had always been perilous. It had to be made at high tide and even medium-draught vessels were sometimes left high and dry on the bottom when the tide ran out. With the big draughts of modern tonnage it became indispensable for the survival of Bristol's maritime trade to build a new port on the mouth of the Avon. At the time of our berthing there it was already quite large and very busy.

We were to be towed by a tug the whole way from Falmouth to Avonmouth, a distance of approximately 260 miles. This illustrates the huge waste of time and effort afflicting the operation of sailing vessels compared to engine-driven ones, which contributed to the final demise of sail shipping.

One of the great disadvantages of wind-powered vessels, especially in a commercial environment, was the uncertainty of arrival time. With the best possible crew and the most experienced captain, a sailing vessel remained dependent on the whim of the elements. Consequently the arrangements for discharge of the cargo could not be made in advance and the vessels could not be directed speedily to the most convenient and economical discharge port. A sailing fleet thus always remained handicapped by old *ad hoc* methods of maritime commerce.

If we had had two-way radio contact with our shipping agents we could have given them our day-to-day position and on the basis of this information they could, to a certain degree, have estimated a very rough date of arrival. On the knowledge of that date it would have been possible to coordinate the arrival and discharge operations. In the best case, we could even have been advised of our orders port while still at sea and saved many days of sailing by going straight there and taking a tow for berthing just off the port.

But in fact, even with such an advantage it would probably not have made a great difference because modern stevedoring demands long-term forward booking and contractual hiring of infrastructure, labour and warehousing. So unless the vessel belonged to a company that controlled these factors itself, it was essential that arrival at a discharge berth of any booked vessel happened on time, otherwise a penalty was forfeited unless a legitimate excuse could be given. In this modern age the excuse that there was no wind to propel the vessel had no validity.

As it was, our owner and the agents took the only commercially viable course available to them under the conditions prevailing. They were faced with the problem of finding a port that would accept our cargo at short notice. To get us there on time meant that, wherever the final destination was, we would have to be towed all the way. Besides, safety considerations alone would have justified this decision. It would have been unwise to send a large unwieldy sailing vessel on a coastal trip in autumn, the gale season, with the possibility of getting onto a lee shore or colliding with another vessel in the busy and, in those years, free-for-all shipping lanes.

The *Viking* had made the long tow along the Channel then round to the West India docks in London. For us Avonmouth was chosen either because the Government Grains Board wanted our cargo there, or because the overall cost of towing and port facilities was the lowest possible.

*

Mike Ruffhead and our 'Commander' Dinty Moore got permission to go ashore on the master's launch to see their relatives who had come down to the port. I was allowed to take advantage of this opportunity though I forget the reason I gave to get permission. Once ashore I went straight to have a haircut. Then I had a look around this old West Country seaport.

The town, situated on the mouth of the River Fal, was built up from the sea-wall terrace, one street above the other. From the sand and pebble beach, uncovered at low tide, steps led up through the wall to the lower streets, then steep alleys or again steps gave access to the higher street levels. In the bottom streets, by the sea wall, were situated most of the shops and ale houses. I visited a couple of ale houses or pubs. One I remember had a drinking cellar and was called 'Chain Locker'; another was called 'The Bull Pit'.

This trip on *terra firma* was short and it was back to the jetty to catch the launch out to our gaunt-looking 'floating palace'. Viewed from the launch our home looked the epitome of the big ocean-going four-poster finally at rest after the long-haul voyage halfway around the world. Much of the paint on the topsides above the waterline had been stripped away by the seas and the bare steel plates bled rust colour all around our hull. However above this stark appearance our rigging looked great. The harbour stow of the sails and the precise trim of the yards, with all lowering ones stopped at the same level on all masts and with all yards braced exactly at the same angle to the mast, would have shown to any old 'sea salt' with a critical eye that things were still done in 'Bristol fashion' aboard this apparition from bygone days.

Both ashore and back aboard I adopted a blasé attitude, as if unaffected by the dramatic transition from toiling for months at sea to walking the streets of a bustling town in my homeland. It was all a show naturally. I wanted to give the impression of a seasoned sailor, but secretly I was boiling with excitement to be home at last after such a seemingly everlasting voyage.

The next day at anchor we received more mail by the launch that came out with fresh bread, milk and other needed stores. We carried on our duties, which were finishing off painting around the deck fittings. I was, as were a few others, sorry to be towed around to Avonmouth instead of going to discharge in London like the *Viking*. Such luck would have been all too much for me to expect.

The third day at anchor was a Saturday and we were still waiting for the tug that was to tow us around to the Bristol Channel. Early that morning we started on the job of sending down the high sails. Apparently, it had been estimated that the lower sails, topsails and courses were enough to hold us to a course and to manoeuvre out of any difficulty if we had to let go the tug towing us or if the towline parted. The reason for stripping the sails off her was, as explained before, to prevent the deterioration of the canvas by toxic pollutants when in port for a long time. We had been informed that unless another cargo was obtained by the time our grain was discharged, we would go into lay-up, with the crew being paid off this time, unlike what had happened in South Africa.

After rigging a gantline at each mast's truck, the royals and topgallants came down in good time and eight bells for midday was being struck as I was bringing down the mizzen gantline block. We were dismissed on this occasion at noon instead of the usual 1pm Saturday knockoff time.

In the afternoon we were entertained by quite a few boatloads of sightseers coming out to the anchorage to get a close-up view of us. As Falmouth, like Cork in Ireland, was a historical port of call for sailing ships, such a sight would have evoked nostalgic pre-war memories for many older citizens of this town.

There were large yachts anchored near us and some of our fellows braved the cold water of the harbour and diving in swam out to one of these craft that had a few woman aboard. But they had no luck at conquests and were not even invited onboard to pursue their interest.

The Customs officers also paid us a visit that afternoon and they did a routine check of the ship's papers and the obligatory search for contraband. Later that evening our tug arrived, from London we were told. We made it fast alongside till the morning. It was the same tug that had towed the *Pamir* up the Thames.

On Sunday 10th October at 6am, the anchor was hove up after the tug had given us its towline and we had made this fast to the forecastle bitts. We were under way on our final lap. We had the forenoon watch and when clear enough of the bay we catted the anchor we had used.

When the wind became favourable we set all the staysails and the spanker to assist the tug and to better control our steering, for our wheel was necessary so that our rudder prevented us from yawing at the end of the tug's towline.

The tow was approximately 260 miles: it took us around the Lizard, then across and around Lands End, along the Atlantic coasts of Cornwall and Devon up to Hartland Point near Bideford Bay, then on up to Bull Point where we swung onto an easterly course up to the Bristol Channel.

The whole passage took two days but was uneventful. Even the weather was kind. For most of the trip our staysails were used to effect. But except for sheeting these home to the side favourable to the wind and hauling over the spanker when necessary, we had no sailing work to perform.

Only one helmsman was necessary. Another man stood by the bitts forward in case our tow had to be cast off in an emergency. The rest of us carried on our normal maintenance work till early on Tuesday morning when we arrived at the breakwater off Avonmouth docks.

After three hours of pushing and pulling assisted by an extra tug, and the use of a line that we sent ashore and heaved in on our capstan, we warped ourselves into position at the discharge berth where two cranes were waiting. Our last real job was to cockbill the three lower yards, trim the rest out of the way and finally let the lower forestays go at the hatches where the cranes were to work first, so they could jib in and out and also luff around to the wharf. The gangs of dockers came aboard and work began to discharge at last the bags of grain that we had transported safely from Australia.

My sister came down from London to see me and came aboard that afternoon. She was quite an attraction to the lads who of course all wanted to know who she was. We had a good talk and she explained what had happened in the family and the reasons why. She had unfortunately to return to her work in London on the next day and so departed early.

The next day my mother arrived. She had come from the Sussex coast via London also by train, but at least was to stay the night at a boarding house. I was stupidly a bit self-conscious and tried to refrain from showing any emotion in front of others, but when we were alone I gave her a big hug and kiss. She had a cry and I nearly did too, seeing her after such a long time and knowing her sad predicament.

After leaving my father she had boarded for some time, but being without money she eventually had to go to live with her own mother and her elder sister Edith who had moved down to Selsey, south of Chichester on the Bill. My grandmother was in a wheelchair and Auntie Edith looked after her. My mother's health was not too good and therefore she could not work. I felt of course very bad that I could not help her out with the pittance I had earned. She said however that if I could afford the fare and if I could get leave she would love me to come and stay at Selsey for at least a week.

She told me that the King Edward VII Navigation School, with which I had started a course for second mate's certificate, was able to accept me as a full-time student. It would take me six months roughly at the school to bring me up to the level of a third-year apprentice so that I could go back to sea again in that position after obtaining such with an employer. Her advice was to pay off the vessel, take a short leave with her, then go up to London and enter the nautical school.

The next day I went to see the master and gave him the stipulated 24 hours notice of termination of my employment. This period however extended to 72 hours owing to delays with money transactions and the shipping office regulations.

Over those next two days I did little work and finished both days at noon. I went up to Bristol on the bus with Martin and Terry and we had a good look around the city. Things were still very austere and areas of the city had acres of vacant space as a result of the heavy German bombing during the war. But we found the locals in high spirits and busy making a success of the post-war export drive.

We visited a ship's chandler's which, we had been told, had the last old-style sail loft left in Britain. In its heyday it had fitted out several famous vessels. Luckily the firm had escaped the bombs. We were shown around by the manager who was very interested when we mentioned we were off the *Passat*. Their orders nowadays were mainly for pleasure craft.

I stayed in the city that night. I visited several very lively pubs and enjoyed the company of some very lively West Country ladies who understood the sailor's predicament of being broke until payday.

My money was depleting fast and on pay-off day I had little to collect. What there was had to keep me in food and accommodation for the next two or three weeks. So the farewell drinks I had with my shipmates were partaken in a pub just near the dock gates at a very short session.

Two years after leaving the English soil, initially to join the *Viking* but ending up on the *Passat*, I carried my gear down the gangway. I transported my sea chest and bag to the gates on a handy wheeler. On showing my pass at the gate, I turned and took a last look at the grand old girl that had been my home and world for those years which had given me a ton of experience.

Turning away to load my luggage into a taxi, I no longer had the same feeling of excitement as when I set out to join her, but instead had one of apprehension as to what the future would be.

Events unfolded quickly. On reaching London I booked into the Sailors' Society Home in Limehouse, opposite West India Dock Road. I found that I could indeed enrol at the navigation school for six months but that I would have to find my own accommodation. It meant therefore boarding and feeding myself at the Society's home for that period. This notorious flophouse, known as the 'stack of bricks', was not the most luxurious but it would have done for me after two years in the *Passat*'s forecastle. The trouble was that I did not have the money for such a long stay even though the weekly rates were very cheap. I would only have enough for two weeks after I came back from the intended stay with my mother. My only option seemed to be to go back to sea as quickly as possible so as to build up a bank and then try again for the school.

There was an unexpected snag, however. Back in June 1946, to go to sea in the Merchant Navy, as they had renamed the service during the war, I had gone through the formal channels used by all entrants, except that I did not go to the national training school. The administration at Dock Street had put me through a medical, including an eyesight test, then on my parents' declaration allowing me to sign on, I had been issued with the usual British Seaman's identity card and a discharge book.

To go back to sea again on British ships, I had to re-enter the system. But the British Federation wanted to know where I had been for the last two years, as the only record they had was of my signing on the *Serenity*. They wanted to see my discharge book, which of course I could not produce, having lost everything in the north Atlantic hurricane, except my passport which was in the master's custody.

The bureaucracy was not interested in this hurricane story, neither had they heard of the *Passat*, or any other sailing ship for that matter. As far as they could see, I was a maverick who had wandered out of the system and had gone on foreign ships, which I suppose was sacrilege to them. On paying off the

Passat, I had been given no discharge, so all I could show was my Finnish Seaman's pay book, or *motbok* as it was called.

My case was fortunately passed up to a higher official, who was prepared to believe my story. They telegraphed the shipping authorities in Helsinki and apparently were supplied with my particulars. And so, after a stern lecture on the dangers of not conforming, I was accepted back into the system as an adult, with the provision that I had to prove my competency to sail on deck before I was allowed to join a British-registered vessel.

I had therefore to button my pride and complete a week's course for the certificate of 'efficient deck hand' (or EDH) on board a training ship called the *Trident* which was moored in the West India Dock. It turned out to be a breeze and a laugh, but then I was told I had to have a lifeboat certificate as well. This was another BOT regulation for seamen after two years' service. So I did a second week there to get this certificate. After another year's service I was to be eligible to sail as an AB and after another year receive full AB's wages of 24 pounds per month. That sounded like a fortune compared to my past pay, so it was an incentive.

While I was obtaining these certificates, I applied to the Gustav Erikson Company in Finland for proper authentication of my service, and I received official documents from them in due course.

Meanwhile, I was leading a very stark existence at the Sailors' Home with only the breakfast they supplied and an evening meal I ate in a cheap café, as I had to save in order to be able to go to see my mother and return to London to find work.

I passed the examinations with no problem, and was immediately off to Victoria Station. I took the train to Chichester and from there a bus down to Selsey. I had a very pleasant but awfully quiet week at my mother's and auntie's place. I paid them a small sum to help with the extra food needed for myself. I went to Chichester for the day once with my mother. I told her all about my travels and about her brother Dick and his family and Uncle George. She was very happy to have me around for that week.

Then it was back to London and once again to the Sailors' Home. I registered for work at the Royal Docks pool this time as the up-river pool at Dock Street catered mainly for short run jobs to the continent or for the home trade. The West India Dock pool would have been alright too, but the Royal Docks pool catered for a far greater variety of jobs on ships going to the four corners of the world. I had my customary medical and was issued with another discharge book.

I then went to several docks and aboard several ships. On these ships I saw the chief mate, asked if there were any jobs and presented my papers. On the second day I secured a job on an Elder Demster Line cargo ship that was loading for the West African coast and the Canary Islands.

I had now made the switch from life under sail and was off for a career in steam, but that's another story.

EPILOGUE

What happened to the *Passat* and the other square-riggers mentioned in this story?

After I left the *Passat*, she fully discharged her cargo at Avonmouth and succeeded to secure another contract with the British Ministry of Food's grain board to transport a further cargo of bagged grain from Port Victoria. So she made another full round voyage, out and back to the UK via Cape Horn.

At the same time the *Pamir*, another of Erikson's fleet and also originally a Flying P Line vessel, went over from New Zealand to load grain in Port Victoria on a similar contract.

She had been interned by New Zealand in 1940, and throughout the war she had been run by the Union SS company, mainly for trips across the Pacific to the west coast of the USA. Now she was being handed back to Erikson as she was no longer a viable proposition for that company. In fact, she had suffered a large financial loss in her last voyage, a round trip to the UK, being laid up in the Shadwell Basin, London docks, for a long time before securing a return cargo to Wellington.

Both now loaded the last cargoes contracted by a European shipowner to be carried in a pure sailing vessel. In mid-1949 they completed loading together but *Pamir* sailed first for Penarth in Wales, taking 127 days on the passage. *Passat* left a few days later but arrived at Penarth before the other, taking 110 days. After discharge both vessels were laid up and used by the Ministry of Food as floating granaries.

Eventually they were bought by German shipping concerns, coming back to their country of origin. In 1951 they were vastly modified and fitted out with auxiliary engines and various modern improvements, such as derricks and Samson posts, generators for electrical power, radar and other navigation instruments. Ballast tanks and new bulkheads were also installed. All this meant that neither could now be classed as a sailing vessel even though their main propulsion was still wind power.

Until 1957 they carried general cargo down to Argentina and grain cargoes in bulk back to north Germany. Accommodation had also been made on them so as to carry sixty cadets each to be trained in sail for the German merchant marine.

All this grand enterprise came to a sudden end when the *Pamir* turned over and sank with the loss of 80 lives, mostly cadets, whilst traversing a hurricane in the low latitudes of the north Atlantic. The *Passat* was also caught in the same blow, but although she was at one time put on her beam ends she was able to right herself by flooding one the newly built ballast tanks and so survived the ordeal.

A marine enquiry found that sailing vessels could no longer be considered safe enough to be employed in the commercial trade of Germany. The *Passat* was consequently laid up in Travemünde, NE of Hamburg, where she still remains as a stationary sail training ship.

The finding of the enquiry was in my opinion a cover for the real cause of the accident. The prime factor contributing to the loss of *Pamir* was the abandonment of the age-old rule that sailing vessels should never carry bulk cargoes. The bulkheads and ballast tanks which had been constructed on the vessels were insufficient to prevent a bulk cargo from shifting within the hold when the vessel was heeled over by the wind in heavy weather conditions.

It was a clear case of overconfidence in the capacity of technological solutions to overcome natural obstacles standing in the way of profit-making. The decision to load grain in bulk had been made on financial grounds, as the handling of bags at both ends of a voyage is time and labour expensive. The real cost, however, was 80 lives, sacrificed to economic efficiency, and it could have been more if the *Passat* had suffered the same fate.

I went aboard my old ship *Passat* as a visitor in 1992 and contemplated how long she would have lasted in that trade under the conditions described above if she had not been retired. There has been talk of putting the old girl into a dry dock to renew the defective plates and other deteriorated parts so as to re-register her as an ocean-going vessel with built-in accommodation in the 'tweendecks to carry passengers. The idea was to make cruises around the Baltic and even further afield during the summer months. However the financial backing for this project seems difficult to secure.

This tragic end of European sail trading left only the Chilean four-mast barque *Omega* (ex British *Drumcliff*) still in service, carrying guano. She was the very last pure commercial sail vessel to ply the ocean, but by 1958 she too was gone, having been wrecked on an island off a lee shore.

The old *Lawhill*, who was first to leave when the three of us loaded at Port Victoria in 1948, was laid up on her return to Cape Town and her South African crew paid off. She was eventually sold to the Portuguese who had ideas of trading with her from East Africa. She was sailed round and anchored in the river near Lourenço Marques, now Maputo, in Mozambique, still then a colony of Portugal. The new owners did nothing with her and finally ran out of money, leaving her to rot away at anchor in that river. I saw her there in 1950, a sorry sight, with her tophamper collapsed on all her masts. She was a total wreck. So ended another grand vessel, originally built in the UK in 1896 for the famous Hill Line.

The second to sail from Port Victoria on the occasion mentioned was the *Viking*. She had arrived in Falmouth long before us after a passage of 139 days. She was towed round to the West India Dock, London, to discharge. After unloading she was towed over to Antwerp and her crew was paid off. Laid up there until 1951, she was eventually towed up to Gothenburg where she became a floating hostel and navigation school for Sweden's merchant marine cadets. To my knowledge she still serves that function.

Finally, the *Pommern* (ex *Mneme*) which I had seen and visited uninvited in Mariehamn at the time I went to join Erikson's, never sailed after the war. Built in Great Britain in 1903, she served in Laeisz's Flying P Line for the nitrate trade. She passed to the Greek Government as reparations at the end of the First World War and was later acquired by Gustav Erikson. She was one of the three vessels that the latter wanted to fit out and trade from Mariehamn in 1946. However the shortage of spare rigging and sails and the lack of finance to purchase such, amongst other difficulties, prevented her from joining the *Viking* and *Passat* on that enterprise.

After old Gustaf died his son Edgar who inherited the firm tried to carry on with both sail and steam vessels. But soon the world's shipping recovery made cargoes for sail impossible to procure, and by 1950 it was realised that sailing ships were definitely no longer economical. After selling the other two vessels to Sweden and to Germany, Edgar Erikson decided to donate the beautiful four-mast barque to the town of Mariehamn.

Here she still lies, as a wonderful example of the love and lasting devotion of the Ålanders for their sailing tradition. She has been on a few occasions towed across to Stockholm when dry-docking was necessary. Otherwise she is kept in top condition by local volunteers, mainly retired seamen, several of whom served aboard this vessel and others sailing from Mariehamn.

As for the other survivors of the First World War, *Priwall*, who was granted to Chile as reparations, caught fire and sank off the Chilean coast in 1945, whereas *Padua* and *Kommodore Johnsen* (ex *Magdalene Vinnen*) went to Russia, being renamed *Kruzenshtern* and *Sedov*, had engines fitted and became training ships for that country's Ministry of Shipping. Both are still in service today. The *Peking*, another survivor from the Flying P Line, is now permanently berthed at the South Street Seaport in New York City.

*

What of the seafarers who manned these sailing vessels?

At the outbreak of the First World War there were few British or American seafarers who specifically stuck to sailing vessels to earn their living. These countries' shipping firms had already mostly changed over to steam. No sailing carriers were built in the UK any more, and if some new sail tonnage was built in the USA they were soft wood fore-and-afters and represented only a small percentage of the nation's tonnage.

There were more sail-trained seamen in the Scandinavian countries, Germany and France, for these countries until then had not made the switch to steam to the same extent and were still replacing old sail tonnage with new buildings.

So at this period British and American sailing vessels were often filling their forecastles with crews, the majority of which were foreigners. However all officers were still nationals.

The war caused so much devastation in the fleets of sailing ships that when normal trading resumed, after the armistice, the seafarers who preferred to ship under sail found it hard to find jobs.

From then only France and Germany built new square-rigged vessels. The last in France was launched in 1919, and when the government bounty subsidy finished with the beginning of the world depression, French shipowners had to dispose of the rest of their sailing fleets. The last the Germans built were, as has been mentioned, the *Priwall* in 1919 and *Padua* in 1926. The German Rickmers company also built some unusually rigged tonnage with auxiliary power after the war.

The opportunity to ship under sail was therefore dwindling for those before the mast, and naturally also the opportunity for budding officers to acquire time in sail for their certificates. In fact Britain had long abandoned the requirement of time spent in sail for their officers of the Merchant Service.

As a matter of fact, except for a few die-hard old shellbacks, professional seamen were no longer lured to sail. One of the main reasons was the length of the voyages and the tenure of articles. All seamen on articles were normally bound for a period of two years or until the vessel returned to the country of registry. But with sailing vessels this could mean several years of tramping around the world before official release could be made. The only other way out was to 'skin out' (desert). Gone were the days of regular runs out to the colonies and back to the home port.

Wages in sail were no better than in steam whereas the difference in work conditions had become very marked. Steamships' men, from the 1930s, worked a three-watch system of only eight hours per day. All hours worked over that were paid at overtime rates. Sailing ships' men still worked on a two-watch system of twelve hours per day and often had to work many supplementary hours when the safety of the ship demanded, with no overtime payment.

In addition, the food and accommodation had become far superior on steamships. Fresh water was plentiful and could be had hot at any time for washing the body or clothes.

By the 1930s, apart from the master and mates, the last sailing vessels were crewed by only a couple of older hands in the forecastle and as petty officers. The rest were boys, most of whom were on articles so as to get a sail endorsement, still necessary in some countries at that time, when they sat for their navigation exams. This was pretty much the situation that I experienced on the *Passat*.

*

With the demise of sail went what constituted a large part of seamanship in the old days. The sailorising skills accumulated over the centuries on wooden vessels rigged with rope fibre cordage were already almost lost with the advent of iron ship building and the fabrication of steel wire rope. With the eventual total abandonment of sail in commercial trade such skills have all but disappeared and will be completely forgotten when the last seafarers who practised them pass on.

Ships no longer have any masts at all, or have only short free-standing ones without staying. Shipboard derricks to work cargo have long disappeared. Nowadays wire rope is spliced ashore under contract and delivered aboard with a certificate of safety. Those who make these wires and perform rigging jobs are shore workers who have never been to sea.

No longer does a worker on a modern vessel carry a knife and a spike. It is a totally different world now at sea and I feel that the opportunity for a lad to make it his life profession with the rewarding sense of mastering unique prestigious skills has gone. Certainly, the forgotten skills have been replaced by a whole range of new, quite sophisticated techniques, and young people choosing a naval career today can still be proud of their achievements. But I wonder if they can have the same sense of belonging to the sea as we had on Old Erikson's square-riggers.

Shipping has now become an industrial enterprise as any other. The shipping industry, of course, has always been run for profit, and shipowners have always been viewed as moneygrubbers, by their crews especially (Erikson first and foremost!). But the international corporatism which has evolved to govern maritime trade as all other industries has resulted in the total subservience of national pride to economic considerations. Countries with a long seagoing tradition no longer have their own mercantile marine or training program. They employ ships from any nationality at the lowest cost possible, often ships from cosmopolitan companies flying flags of convenience that hire cheap, mostly untrained skeleton crews and minimally trained officers to navigate from A to B. Few vessels now fly a national flag. Their anonymous owners have no allegiance to any nation but only to the Global Dollar.

*

The great achievements of ship-builders and seafarers over the centuries are quickly falling into oblivion. Bemoaning the devaluation of the seafaring life brought about by the unstoppable pace of progress, I feel I sound like an embittered grumpy old man fixated on fantasised memories. It is indeed a great temptation to idealise the past. Admittedly, much is gained through economic and technical progress. But much is lost also, in human terms. The life of the sea was a culture of its own.

I have seen a great and enthralling chapter of human history close in the very short period of one lifespan. This story has been about this transition.

APPENDIX 1

BALLAST: ITS HANDLING AND CARRIAGE ON SAILING VESSELS

The lay person is often not aware of the complexity of the question of ballasting in the operation of cargo vessels, if aware at all of the very necessity for ballast.

Ballast is, simply put, extra weight placed in a vessel in order to increase its stability. Many sea-going vessels, for instance pleasure craft or service craft of all sorts, never need ballasting operations because they are built with a low centre of gravity (usually achieved with permanent ballast such as lead or cast iron lugs affixed to the keel or the bottom of the hull) and the weight of their load (e.g. passengers and provisions) is not large in relation to the weight of their structure. Their total weight, and therefore their displacement, and the position of their centre of gravity never vary much in normal use of the vessels.

A cargo ship on the other hand is specifically designed to carry the maximum payload achievable given its size, and its total weight will vary greatly depending on the amount of cargo it carries. The draught of the vessel, and consequently its freeboard, will vary accordingly. This variation was in fact even more important in sailing vessels, which had relatively narrow hulls in order to optimise their sailing ability, than in modern steamers which have larger beams.

It is clear that there is a limit to the weight of the cargo that can be safely taken on board. Sufficient freeboard must be preserved so that water does not reach over the sides and inundate the structure, even when the vessel is rolling or listing. For all vessels built and registered for the carriage of commercial goods, this safety limit is determined in accordance with strict guidelines issued by the UK Board of Trade and now endorsed by international marine code, and indicated by a load line mark stamped on the hull. When a vessel is 'down to her mark' no more cargo may be loaded.

There is however a second safety limit. On many occasions vessels will not be full of cargo to submerge them to their load line. They will often be only half full, and on many voyages, especially on bulk cargo trades and when tramping, they will in fact be empty or 'light ship' en route to a loading destination. In this condition, in fact whenever the quantity of cargo has been reduced past a certain minimum, the vessel will become top heavy and unstable, unless a compensatory weight is loaded in order to lower its centre of gravity.

If ever the centre of gravity was allowed to rise above the centre of buoyancy (the average point where the upward thrust of the water applies) the vessel would capsize. Moreover, the centre of buoyancy is dependent on the shape of the submerged part of the structure, and continually shifts horizontally and vertically with the movements of the vessel. Consequently, a vessel may seem stable when on a more or less even keel, but in fact be so 'tender' that capsizing conditions are reached when it is heeled over to one side by an external force (sea, wind, tow line, etc.)

In order to maximise the carrying capacity of commercial cargo ships, they are left somewhat tender at construction time. There is no point in crippling them from the start with permanent in-built ballast. Stability will be provided by the weight of the cargo. Prior to the launching of a new vessel the builder supplies the owner with a set of specifications. So as not to have his new vessel 'turn turtle' at the launch the owner uses these to ascertain the amount of initial ballast he has to stow into the bottom of the new building so that it can be safely moved to its fitting-out berth.

From then on those in charge of loading, discharging and sailing the vessel, that is to say the master and his mates, will use the figures, scales and graphs supplied to manage the cargo in such a way that the vessel remains buoyant, stable and seaworthy under all conditions encountered, and the problem of ballasting will be their constant preoccupation.

Here I must impress that for sailing vessels correct ballasting procedures were particularly vital and demanded care and experience. They were subjected, through their sails and tophamper, to wind pressures of considerable weight and leverage that had to be counteracted by important amounts of low-placed ballast. The added weight had to be distributed carefully in order to optimise rather than jeopardise the sailing abilities and manoeuvrability of the vessel. The amount of ballast taken had to be apportioned to the prevailing weather and sea conditions, and also depended on the type of rig carried, the height and weight of the tophamper and the amount of sail one wished to keep on.

Fine judgment was necessary to strike the right compromise between safety and sailing efficiency. The right solution was not always obvious. For example, there were some drawbacks in stowing heavy material very low. A too low centre of gravity, whilst allowing a good sail area, hence a good speed, could result in dangerous heavy rolling.

Again, with an empty ship, there was advantage in carrying as much ballast as possible. Contrary to the expectations of non-sailors, a light ship cannot sail as fast a fully laden one, except in exceptionally weak breezes, since it cannot carry as much canvas when the wind freshens. But a possible increase in sailing abilities had to be balanced against the cost incurred in loading the extra ballast necessary.

A related issue was that by sending down part of the tophamper one could reduce the leverage of the destabilising forces and therefore the amount of ballast needed. But this advantage was of course offset by the loss of sail power. Some vessels sent down the royal yards if crossed, others these plus upper topgallants, more so if a trip in ballast was to be made in regions where the inclement weather and the season precluded to a great extent the setting of such upper sails.

Ballasting operations, as an integral part of cargo management, were no trivial matter, for in addition to technical knowledge and seamanship they required attention to important logistic and economic considerations.

In the heyday of sail, vessels trading to main ports on regular runs often had cargo either way, but even in these ideal conditions it was not always possible to stevedore them in such a way that ballast did not have to be used. This depended on the layout and facilities of the ports visited. Sometimes inward-bound cargo was worked on one side of a river port and outward bound cargo could only be loaded on the other side. Or the wharves for various types of cargo were situated at different places around a harbour. For the shift from wharf to wharf, or from discharging wharf to anchorage and back again when delays intervened, ballast had to be added as soon as the amount of cargo left in the vessel was insufficient to ensure stability. Casualties were common whenever this exercise was neglected. Empty ships left in such condition for a short interval when stevedoring, so as to save costs, have keeled over alongside, those going over to the shore side spearing the wharf sheds with their yards.

From the men's point of view, the best ballast, quite evidently, was any type that was loaded at the wharf by crane, stowed by shore labour, and discharged by the same means. But for the owners and masters, economic factors prevailed. They had to weigh the cost of shore labour in a given port against crew costs and ascertain the availability, proximity and cost of materials and the facilities provided for loading.

A cardinal factor to be included in the equation was the possibility of selling the ballast at the port of destination. Much ballast carried in the early days of settlement in the Americas or the British or other European colonies was used for road or building construction. When possible the most sought after material was used, even scrap metal.

If no resellable materials were available at an advantageous cost then the cheapest material was chosen, having in mind the time and labour that would be involved, how far the vessel would have to travel from its loading berth to load this ballast, how long it would thus be absent, and how the material could be disposed of at the port of destination. The sea floor around many older ports worldwide is covered, sometimes metres deep, with all kinds of ballast materials dumped over the decades by countless ships. The time for one or often several trips to the designated dumping grounds had to be factored into the ship's schedule. All this had to be planned with the same care as the movement of cargo and to obtain all necessary information it was imperative for the owner to have reliable and honest agents in all the ports of his vessels' itinerary.

Ballast was generally in solid form, the most usual being earth-rock mix, stone or rocks, brick chips or sand. It was placed on the bottom of the lower hold in positions where it served to trim the vessel forward or aft so as to obtain the best sailing qualities when under way, taking into consideration the voyage contemplated, the time of year and the weather likely to be experienced.

In general it was stowed in 'blocks' in the square of the hatch. To minimise the stresses put on the structure and to spread the weight enough to perfect the trim, there could be two, three or even four blocks, depending on the hatch access.

Timber brows were built up to form the blocks, allowing cargo to be loaded immediately alongside without contamination. When the ballast was removed, after the equivalent weight in cargo had been stowed, the timber walls were removed leaving an empty space which was also filled up with cargo.

The surface of the stowed ballast was levelled off, and unless it was only taken on for a shift-ship or a short move in sheltered waters, it was securely lashed down with old chain and old heavy wire, often laid over limbers. Another precaution, especially with loose materials, was the building in of longitudinal and thwartship shifting boards as the ballast was stowed, as it was imperative to prevent any shift of the load in heavy seas.

Shifting of ballast on a voyage was extremely perilous. It has been the cause of the loss of many vessels. Some have survived only at the cost of tremendous efforts of their crew working night and day down the hold in suffocating conditions, often in near darkness and with precarious foothold, restowing the ballast by shovelling it 'back up hill' so as to right their vessel.

The exercise of ballasting up to the end of the epoch of sail was practically as primitive as on the earliest traders navigated by man. Even when motorised winches were available, it involved a great deal of manpower.

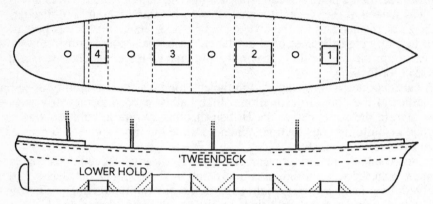

Placement depends on required trim. Most common: hatches N° 2 & 3.
Min. ballast needed on large carriers: • standing in port: 300-400 tons
                                       • coastal voyage: 800-900 tons
                                       • inter-ocean: 1500-1700 tons

PLACEMENT OF BALLAST

As a general rule, the crew handled the ballasting, in and out, except where cheap shore labour was procurable (and it had to be cheap to undercut most crews' wages). In fact, when discharging at a wharf, the shore labour that unloaded the cargo would often also load the ballast with shore equipment out of rail trucks. But occasionally ballast came alongside outboard in lighters, tenders or barge, which was always the case when stevedoring in the stream or roads, and in these circumstances the crew was utilised.

The discharge and dumping of non-resellable ballast was almost always done by the crew. This job was a sailor's nightmare, about the worst he was ever asked to perform. Working day in day out, sometimes in gangs around the clock if time was at a premium, the operation could take five days or more. If there was no immediate hurry then day work would suffice. This was a twelve-hour day, five days per week, with often an extra six hours on Saturday. No extra money was ever paid, for this was not classed as cargo work.

The necessity of ballasting was therefore a phenomenal curse for sail carriers. So much was this a debilitating factor that owners sometimes converted vessels to carry permanent ballast. Although this reduced the quantity of cargo that could be carried, the loss was compensated for by the savings in turn-around time and stevedoring fees in some very competitive trades.

Today all cargo carriers are built with double bottoms and/or other built-in tanks that can accommodate an adequate quantity of liquid ballast for all the various combinations of cargo load and weather conditions that may be encountered. Water is the common material used, although other liquids unlikely to damage the pumping machinery have been used to a financial advantage. With this system the time and cost of the ballasting operations are minimal since they can be carried out as cargo is displaced or loaded. If the material used is sea water, the amount of ballast carried can even be increased or decreased while under way according to the dictates of the weather.

It has however been realised of late that this system is not always as smooth and economical as expected. The drawback of the method is that polluted ballast water can be carried into more pristine regions. Health and marine authorities worldwide, with good reason, exercise increasingly stringent control over the quality of the water used as ballast, and when pollutants are identified on arrival at port all the ballast has to be pumped into a tanker and the owners have to foot the cost of sterilisation.

Only a handful of the later-built sailing vessels, such as the *Viking*, the *Preussen* and *France II*, were fitted with water ballast tanks. But the *Priwall* and the *Padua*, built in 1919 and 1926 respectively and fitted with practically all the modern equipment available at the time, had no water ballasting facilities, even though they had engines that could have worked the pumps. By that time sailing ships had become dinosaurs in other ways, and as they carried non-perishable cargoes that did not require fast time schedules and employed low-wage crews, shipowners did not proceed with the hefty expense of constructing ballast tanks.

Sailing vessels suffered a serious handicap owing to their special needs for ballast and their primitive methods of handling it. It is one of the major factors which brought about the demise of commercial sail. It was obvious that this means of maritime transport could not survive in a world of cut-throat competition where express delivery of merchandise is a paramount requirement.

APPENDIX 2

LOADING AND UNLOADING WITH SHIP GEAR

The method of loading and unloading cargo or ballast with shipboard cargo gear, on sailing vessels, was still rather primitive and time-consuming.

A gin block was slung on spans between the two masts forward and aft of the given hatch, and plumbed over its centre. The cargo runner (constructed of six-strand flexible wire) led off the winch, up through the gin block and down the hatch to the swivel ring above the cargo hook and the proposed lift. From this swivel ring, another runner was led up, out through a block hung off the end of the lower yardarm that was plumbed over the wharf or lighter. This yardarm runner was then led down to the pin-rail barrel known as the 'nok' on the gunwale. This nok was a large log of timber, sheathed with steel plate, bolted to the pin rail.

Discharging Bagged Cargo into Lighters or Barges Using Ships Gear

ELEVATION

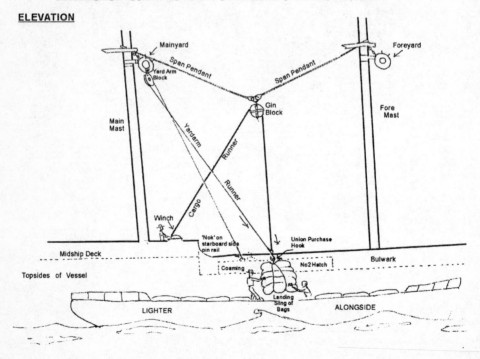

On taking the sling of cargo up from the hatch, the winch would heave it high up to the gin block. The seaman working the yardarm runner, the 'nokman', would take in all the slack on his runner by hand. He would then take about five or six turns of the runner, depending on the weight of the lift, around the nok barrel. The winch would then come back lowering away, and the lift being eased out would swing over the ship's side until it plumbed over the wharf or lighter. The yardarm hand would then have the weight, and surge off his runner on the barrel, lowering the lift away.

The method was therefore very similar to the two-derrick, union purchase system used on most conventional steamships, except that there was no winch for the yardarm runner. The operation was slow, as one can visualise, and the yardarm runner soon ended up full of 'hooks', frayed wire breaks. The use of a mechanical winch and a nok was still a great improvement over the older methods using hand winches, horses or men jumping off a stage and hanging onto either of the runners.

The same procedure with the re-slinging of some of the blocks, and repositioning of the nok onto the outboard hatch coaming, was used for loading from lighters when at anchor in the stream, or in ports with no cranes.

Discharging Bagged Cargo into Lighters or Barges Using Ships Gear

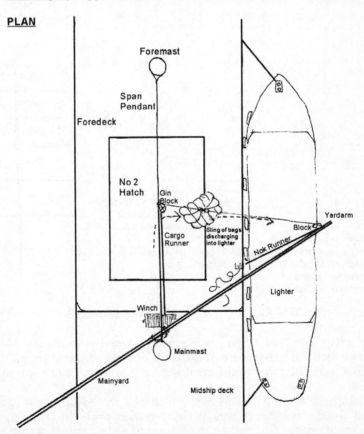

PLAN

Foremast

Span Pendant

Foredeck

No 2 Hatch

Gin Block

Cargo Runner

Sling of bags discharging into lighter

Nok Runner

Yardarm

Block

Lighter

Winch

Mainmast

Mainyard

Midship deck

APPENDIX 3

SAIL CHANGING ON A SQUARE-RIGGED VESSEL

Sails were, understandably, the centre of the square-rigged sailor's existence. Most of his work took place aloft. When he was not setting, furling or changing sail, he was overhauling and maintaining the mass of rigging. In fair weather, watch after watch would be spent at these tasks. In heavy weather a sailor could spend all his watch on deck followed by his watch below still up aloft taking in sail. Back down on deck, if he was not at the helm, he was during daytime watches most often repairing or making new sails, while continuously going about tacking the vessel or just trimming the yards on the braces. The safety of the ship and the life of everyone depended on giving the sail and rigging one's continuous attention.

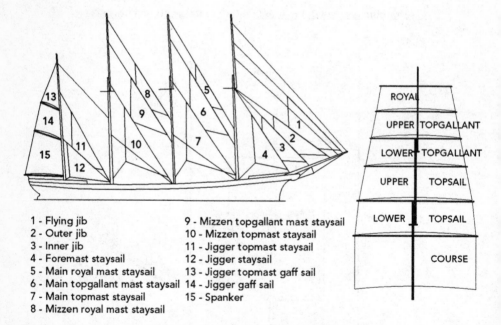

1 - Flying jib
2 - Outer jib
3 - Inner jib
4 - Foremast staysail
5 - Main royal mast staysail
6 - Main topgallant mast staysail
7 - Main topmast staysail
8 - Mizzen royal mast staysail
9 - Mizzen topgallant mast staysail
10 - Mizzen topmast staysail
11 - Jigger topmast staysail
12 - Jigger staysail
13 - Jigger topmast gaff sail
14 - Jigger gaff sail
15 - Spanker

THE SAILS OF A FOUR-MAST BARQUE

In the early days, the larger traders were generally three-mast ship-rigged vessels on which the masts were of different dimensions, as were all the yards. All the sails were therefore of different areas and were cut and sewn to separate patterns.

The competition from steamships, which had the advantage of guaranteed speed and could avail themselves of cheap bunker coal and later oil, started a never-ending drive for cost cutting in all areas of sailing vessel construction and operation.

Significant savings were achieved when at least the fore and main masts were made identical, as well as their respective yards. This allowed for two of each type of sail to be cut and sewn to the same pattern. This incidentally helped the introduction of the three-mast barque. Within a decade many ship-rigged vessels had their yards stripped from their mizzen mast and they too became barques.

With the introduction of the four-mast barque still more saving could be achieved as a suit of sails now consisted of three identical sets of sails for the three square-rigged masts.

The saving was even carried further when owners commissioned more than one vessel of the same dimensions or even a series. Not only could sails be interchanged shipboard but they could now be exchanged from ship to ship and almost mass-produced in the sail loft. And the sailmakers of course kept the patterns for further orders.

A new vessel would always be provided with at least two suits of sails from the sail-making firm engaged by the owner. Sometimes a third suit came later, after the maiden voyage, from the same loft, which had kept all the measurements.

It was actually usual to carry three suits. They first used to be made of different canvas weights, numbered 1–6, for various weather conditions. No.1 or storm canvas was used in all heavy weather. No. 3 was for fluctuating weather, up to strong winds. No. 5 was for trade-wind weather. This practice was discontinued owing to expense. Later all canvas used on general carriers was heavy-duty storm canvas or 00 gauge. So new vessels would be provided with two or three suits of this weight.

Over time, with wear and tear, these suits became graded. After being used for some time in heavy weather a new suit became the second suit, reserved for moderate weather conditions such as the trade winds, and an unused suit was put to duty as the storm set. After a further period a third unused suit became the heavy-weather suit while the other two went down the hierarchy, the first used suit having now deteriorated to the point where it was suitable only for very light breezes and expendable enough to be exposed to the wear and tear of the doldrums situations in the 'horse' latitudes.

This system of rotation preserved the best and strongest suit to stand up to the harshest elements. It entailed, of course, a heavy workload for the crew who had to send down and bend again whole suits of sails several times during each voyage.

Here are some examples of sail-changing patterns on specific voyages around the globe.

North Atlantic, UK to east coast of North America:
Summer, second suit used. No change unless for repairs, replaced by old heavy canvas. Winter, best suit heavy canvas. No change except for repairs, replaced by best heavy canvas.

Europe to west coast of South America:
Heavy suit leaving. Change to second suit on picking up the NE trades around 35–30° N. Change to the oldest patched canvas in the doldrums if becalmed for any lengthy period. Change back to second suit on picking up the SE

trades. Sometimes, with luck, no change was needed between the NE and SE trades. On the SE trades blending into the westerlies around 30–35° S a sail change is made back to heavy-duty sail to beat south and westwards around the Horn, then north up the Pacific coast. This was carried till port unless going to the furthest north Chilean ports when a change could be required again. Unless sailing further up the coast within a short period, all sail was sent down in the loading port.

Europe to Australia or New Zealand:
Heavy-duty suit on leaving Europe unless in good summer conditions when the second suit was carried into the trades, otherwise the change was made on picking up the trades. Again this suit was carried if by luck the trades almost met. If not then the change was made to old patched sail until the SE trades were reached. On meeting the westerlies the change was made back to the best heavy canvas again. This suit was carried running the easting down in the Roaring Forties or even the Filthy Fifties and left on until the southern ports of Australia or those of New Zealand were reached, when all sails were dried and sent down.

Apart from this regular system, changing sail would take place if a sail was torn, rent, split or even blew out, which could always happen in severe wind gusts.

In the days of cheap canvas and cheap labour, all sail would be carried to the last minute and beyond if it was not endangering the sailing ability of the vessel or any other components of the rigging. If a sail blew out before it could be furled, the loss was not great and was more than compensated by the increase in speed achieved over the whole voyage by holding onto sail.

The last company to practise such sail driving was the Laeisz Flying P Line. Their vessels were the strongest-rigged ever built and even in the 1930s the policy was to clap on and hold onto as much sail possible, with due concern for safety, so that two round voyages could be accomplished per year. However Laeisz had an efficient backup organisation in Hamburg, the fleet's home port, including a first-rate firm of sailmakers. They also had sails and other gear stored on the Chilean coast.

But in the final days of sail, owing to the growing running costs, the rule was to furl sail before the point of blowing out was ever reached.

When Erikson fitted out his last two commercial sailing vessels after the Second World War, he had to cannibalise his older vessels and use sails from his shore stores that had not been in use for five years. There were few bolts of canvas in Finland from which to cut new sails. The instruction given to the two masters was to preserve their sails at all costs. Consequently we never chanced hanging onto sail till the last minute and the exercise of reducing sail at any excuse kept the watches continuously employed on every voyage.

When a sail needed to be changed, the procedure was to wait for a lull in the wind, especially if the vessel was running close hauled and could not be paid off. A few men would go aloft with a block and gantline and would unshackle, cut loose and send down the sail or its remains while the other hands would draw out the replacement from the sail locker. If it was a large sail such as a course (lower sail) or topsail then they would wait for the relief watch to come on deck at the change of watch, otherwise they would send it up, bend it and set it themselves. Sometimes, in heavy conditions, it was essential to replace the sail immediately, for instance to keep way on the vessel if she was under topsails only. Then the watch below was called out at any time. When necessary the dayworkers were also called out to assist, especially when a course was involved. Usually all fore-and-afters were handled immediately by the watch on deck without any help.

To send down a square sail, a tail block was affixed on the forward side of the mast above the sail to be changed. If only one sail was to be changed the block was placed at a height of at least half the length of the yard on which the sail was bent. If all the sails on the mast were to be changed it was made fast at the truck so as to be high enough to change the royal. A gantline was rove through the block, long enough so both ends reached the deck and a little over.

The chosen sail, if it was on a standing yard (lower topsail, lower topgallant yards), would be brailed up by releasing the sheets and heaving on the clew lines and buntlines. If it was on a hoisting yard (upper topsail, upper topgallant, or royal yards) then the halyards of these yards would be let go and the downhauls heaved on, bringing these yards down and brailing up their clews and buntlines plus leechlines if fitted.

The end of the gantline was passed at the bunt, clear of the jackstay, twice around the sail and made fast. Other lashings were passed around at the points of the buntlines and sometimes near the yardarms to envelop the leeches of the sail. The clewline and sheet on each clew were unshackled from the clew cringle iron and temporally reshackled to each other, ready to be shackled back onto the clew iron of the replacement sail.

The buntlines were unshackled or unlashed from the sail's foot and bent back on their own part again temporarily. The same was done with any leechline. Then the head earing lashings each side were let go and the sail was free and ready to drop when the robands[1] were cut free. The heaving end of the gantline was made fast ready to be slacked away. The robands were cut one by one from each yardarm inwards by a hand on each side of the yard. Only two hands were needed aloft when the last robands were cut near the bunt where a few had already been cut to bend the gantline.

---

[1] Robands, also called rovings, were pieces of rope, generally 3½-inch sisal or other cheaper line, cut into approximately 24-inch lengths. The three strands were separated then each strand was halved again. They were passed through holes cut in the head of the sail just below the head boltrope, then around the jackstay three or four times, then around these loops horizontally a few times either way, and finally made fast and their ends neatly cut off. The holes in the head were invested with a grommet sewn in to stop fraying and for extra strength. They were evenly spaced across the head. When a sail was sent up for bending each hole had its roband temporarily hitched in it.

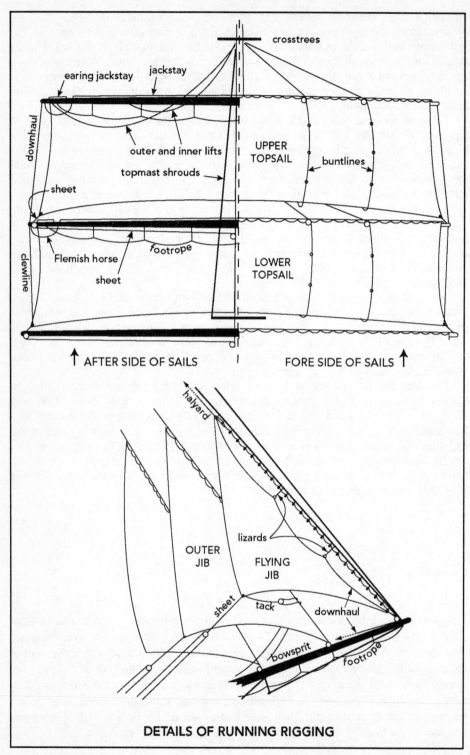

crosstrees

earing jackstay   jackstay

downhaul

UPPER
TOPSAIL

outer and inner lifts

buntlines

topmast shrouds

sheet

clewline

Flemish horse

footrope

sheet

LOWER
TOPSAIL

↑ AFTER SIDE OF SAILS   FORE SIDE OF SAILS ↑

halyard

lizards

OUTER
JIB

FLYING
JIB

sheet   tack

downhaul

bowsprit

footrope

DETAILS OF RUNNING RIGGING

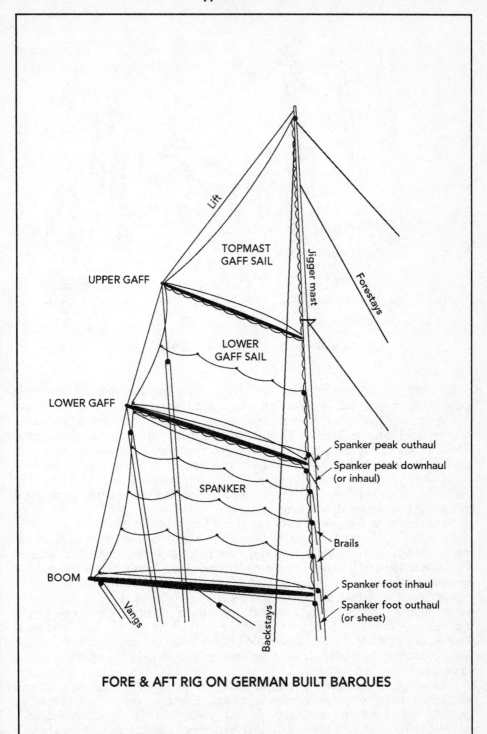

FORE & AFT RIG ON GERMAN BUILT BARQUES

SENDING UP A SAIL ON A GANTLINE

The sail or its remains now hung loose from the gantline, the two ends hanging down doubled. A guide line was made fast to these ends if the vessel was laying over so far as to plumb the sail out over the side when it descended to deck level, or if rolling would cause it to foul any other parts of the rigging. When all was ready the gantline was slacked away and the guideline hauled in until the sail reached the deck, when it was carried to a hatch, or if the well decks were awash the sail was landed on a flying bridge. It was left there until the replacement had been dealt with, and then carried under cover to be dried and, when time allowed, repaired and stowed.

Bending a square sail was straightforward, but time-consuming. The replacement sail brought on deck from the locker was placed forward of the mast on the best side to clear stays and other rigging components, depending on which tack the ship was on. The earing lanyards were bent on each end and the gantline made fast. The heaving end of this line was then taken to a deck capstan via a leadblock and up went the sail by the efforts of up to six or more hands putting their full weight on their capstan bar. When the required height was reached, four of them went aloft to the yard where the sail was to be bent. Two on each side of the yard took hold of an earing lanyard and as the gantline was eased away below, hauled out the earings to the yardarm as the sail's bunt came down level with the yard.

The weight of the made-up sail prevented the head being stretched fully and so gaskets were temporarily passed around it to take the weight. Then the gantline was freed and the hands on the yardarm with the assistance of a handybilly (a small two-and-one tackle) hauled out the earing cringle and put it on the hook affixed to the earing jackstay on the end of each yardarm, and the earing lanyards were rove and hitched. The clewline and sheet were then separated and reshackled onto each clew iron. Next any leechline was affixed to the leech. The buntlines were reeved through their thimbles and shackled on the foot. Working in from the yardarm the robands were put in, made fast and their ends cut.

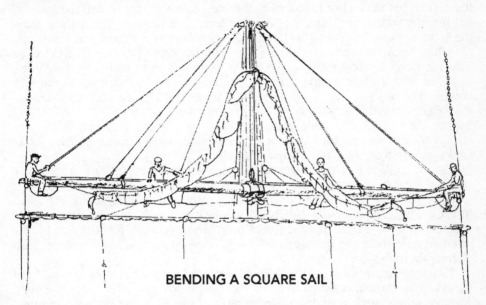

BENDING A SQUARE SAIL

The sail was then ready to be set after the temporary lashings had been cut and the gaskets let go. If the sail was on a travelling yard it was topped, if on a standing yard it was sheeted home. In both instances the buntlines were overhauled and tied off with the usual rope yarn, and the gaskets made up.

With travelling yards there was no clewline and only a standing sheet shackled onto the yard below, for the yard brought down by the downhauls brailed up the sail at the yardarms and only the buntlines had to be hauled tight as the yard came down.

Changing the fore-and-afters was lighter work. The spanker was set by hauling the head peak out to the head of the gaff with the outhaul, which ran through a sheave fitted in the gaff. The weight of the head of the sail was taken by robands rove through head holes and tied to shoes that travelled along a track welded to the underside length of the gaff. The luff, or mast side of the sail, was made fast to a jackstay running down the after side of the mast, again by robands. The foot blew free as did of course the leech. Where these two met was the clew cringle, shackled to the foot outhaul which ran through a sheave set in the end of the boom, and to the foot inhaul which led back to the mast.

To assist in furling the spanker and the gaff topsail, several lines, called brails, were shackled at intervals onto the leech. They ran through blocks on each side of the sail and down to the fife rail. When the peak outhaul and foot outhaul were let go and the head downhaul and foot inhaul plus the brails (three on the spanker, two on the gaff) were heaved on, the sails were brought into the mast and furled or changed.

The jibs and staysails were three-sided sails bent to forestays and they slid up and down these stays by means of metal hanks. The longest side of the sail, the luff, was made fast to these hanks by robands passed through holes cut in the sail below the bolt rope and grommeted. At the point where the leech meets the foot was sewn in the clew cringle to which was shackled both the sheet and the tack. This tack always led over the stay below or aft to the lee side, to become the sheet when going on the other tack. To send down the sail was easy: the halyards were let go and the downhaul heaved on as the sheet was eased off.

When bending such sails, the halyard and the downhaul were shackled on then the robands were rove on the hanks. Next the sheet and lazy sheet were shackled on the clew cringle. Last the standing tack was shackled on the tack cringle. The sail was hauled up the stay by the halyard till the tack was taut and the sheet trimmed in to gain the sail its maximum advantage.

The fore-and-afters were generally easy to change, although there was always the chance of a foul-up with a halyard or downhaul coming adrift, or the hanks jamming on the way down or even up.

The topgallant and royal staysails, however, were exceptions. They were bent onto stays the lower ends of which fastened onto the after side of the mast forward. To bend, unbend or furl these sails meant working on footropes called 'horses' stretched between the backstays, where one's footing was a little precarious for jobs requiring the use of both hands. Another difficult set, for the same reason, were the spanker and the gaff or upper spanker fitted on most German-built vessels.

I have not mentioned sails with reef bands and accessories. We did not have these on the *Passat* as they had been superseded on the modern square-rigger. They could be handled with the large crews of old days, but with the minimal crews which manned the heavy-rigged steel vessels they were no longer practical. The same goes for stunsails or studding sails which used to be bent on booms that extended outboard of the yards, and skysails and even moonrakers which were set above the royals.

Generally all sails were sent down in port, but when the stay would only be very short the sails were left bent in a neat harbour stow. However great attention was paid then to the possibility of damage to the canvas caused by contamination from toxic cargo handled in the port. On the Chilean coast the dust rising from the nitrate when loading could accumulate in the folds of bent sails and react with rain water with disastrous effect on the sailcloth.

Sails were always dried before being stowed away, if possible before they were sent down. All sails were marked above the clew cringles for easy identification when taken out. If possible any sail needing repairs was attended to before stowing. If there was no time for this, it was put aside until time was made. The sail locker was set out with racks and the sailmaker meticulously organised the stowage of each sail in its correct place. His was one of the key jobs on board and he was constantly occupied stowing, maintaining, repairing, renewing the sails on which the vessel's survival depended.

Some new sails were actually made by hand on board. As a matter of fact it had become difficult to have correctly fitting sails made ashore by specialised companies.

Up to 1900 the balance had not tipped to a serious degree in favour of steam. There was still a demand for the growing of flax in Ireland, cotton in the USA and jute in India, a great proportion of which was fabricated into bolts of canvas and purchased by shipowners. Sail-making was still a prosperous industry employing many skilled workers around the world.

But the First World War saw the almost total demise of sail. Sailmakers went out of business or diverted. Eventually the skills of this trade were lost ashore as loft foremen, cutters and hands were paid off never to be replaced. The art of sail-making was kept alive at sea where, owing to these circumstances, more sails were made than ever before. Sails made in the last shore lofts that remained in business gradually deteriorated in cut and fit and were never as good as shipboard-made sails.

One consoling fact is that the art is still alive today, and has even been improved in some respects, thanks to the ever-increasing popularity of pleasure craft.

GLOSSARY

Articles (of agreement): contract between shipowners and crew.

Barque-rigged: with fore-and aft sails on the aftermost mast, and square sails on all the others.

Beam: the pieces of the framework of a ship running from side to side and supporting the decks. A vessel 'on her beam ends' is listing 90° on her side (and likely to capsize). By extension, the width of the hull.

Belay: (vb) to stop and secure a running line around a cleat or a belaying pin.

Belaying pin: a metal bar fitting in a rail which serves as a cleat.

Bell: a bell is kept on the forecastle head to signal various conditions and to indicate time. Throughout the full 24 hours it is struck every half hour. Eight strokes signal the change of watches, hence the expression 'at eight bells'.

Bend: (vb) to attach with a hitch or knot. To fasten a sail to its yard.

Binnacle: box holding the compass placed on a stand near the steering wheel.

Boatswain's chair or **Bos'n's chair**: a short plank suspended by bridles affixed to its corners on which a person can sit to work aloft or over the sides of a ship.

Bogey: stove.

Boltrope: a reinforcing rope sewn round the edges of a sail.

Boot topping: the area of a ship's sides between the high and the low water marks. It is painted with anti-fouling paint, usually a different colour from the rest of the hull.

Bowline: a loop made at the end of a rope with a non-slipping knot.

Braces: lines attached to the yardarms and used to adjust the orientation of the yards in the horizontal plane.

Brails: ropes used to gather in a fore-and-aft sail into the mast. 'To brail in (or up) a sail' is to gather a fore-and-aft sail with its brails, or by extension gather up a square sail to its yard.

Broach to: (vb) to veer and present the side of the vessel to the wind and waves.

Bulkhead: an upright partition.

Bulwarks: the part of the ship's side extending above the level of the deck and forming a protective fence.

Bunt: middle part of a sail.

Buntline: rope attached to the foot of a square sail and passing in front of the sail to a block on the yard. Used to pull up the bottom of the sail. They have to be regularly 'overhauled', that is, adjusted so as not to restrain or rub against the sail when the latter is filled with wind.

Cable: the anchor's cable, whether chain, fibre or steel rope.

Castle: an elevated part of a ship above the upperdeck (e.g. forecastle, centre or midship castle, poop).

Cat: (vb) to secure an anchor to its cathead.

Catheads: short beams projecting on each side of the bowsprit where anchors are temporarily suspended.

Ceiling: the internal planking of a ship, especially (and confusingly for the layman) the wooden flooring at the bottom of the hold.

Chippy or **Chips**: familiar name for a ship's carpenter.

Clew: lower corner of a sail.

Coamings: the planks forming a raised border around a hatch.

Cockbill: (vb) to tip a yard out of the horizontal.

Course: one of the large lower sails.

Cross: (vb) to send up and attach a yard to a mast.

Crossjack or **cro'jack**: lower sail on the mizzen mast (or its yard).

Crosstrees: in general usage, a construction at the junction of lower and upper masts, which comprises a small semi-circular platform. Technically, the term only refers to the thwartship spars supporting the platform.

Davits: the curved pillars close to the vessel's side from which the boats are suspended.

Deck head: the underside of a deck above one's head (the 'ceiling' in common language).

Dog watch: two short watches, 4–6pm and 6–8pm, introduced to avoid keeping the same watch hours for each team from day to day.

Downhaul: rope used to haul down a jib or staysail.

Fairlead: any fitting with a hole through which running lines are guided.

Fid: a wooden tapered tool used in splicing cordage.

Fife rails: racks for belaying pins situated around the foot of the masts.

Flush decker: a vessel with no centre castle.

Footrope: a rope fastened with stirrups to the underside of a yard on which men stand when working on that yard.

Forecastle: (1) the foremost elevated part of a vessel. (2) the crew's quarters, not necessarily under the forecastle head. (3) the crew, excluding the officers.

Forepeak: the forward part of the hold, forming a separate compartment used for stores.

Freeing ports: hinged panels cut into the strakes above the deckline. Held by a restraining chain, they open outwards to an angle of approximately 45 degrees, thus allowing fast drainage of the decks.

Furl: to gather a sail, roll it up and fasten it to its yard with gaskets.

Gantline: a line rove through a block temporarily attached to a mast or stay and used for hoisting sails, spars, etc.

Gaskets: lengths of rope used to secure a furled sail to the yard.

Gin block: a kind of heavy-duty metal block, especially used for cargo.

Gipsy: a horizontal barrel on the forecastle head used in hauling anchor cables. It is powered by the capstan or by the donkey engine via the windlass and has specially shaped grooves snuggly fitting the links of the chain which is laid over it.

Gunnel or **gunwale**: upper edge of the ship's sides. Practically the top of the bulwarks.

Halyard or **halliard**: permanent line used to hoist a sail or a yard.

Hawse pipes: the pipes through the bow of the vessel up which the cables run from the anchors to the capstan or windlass.

Heave to: (vb) to stop a vessel by bringing her head to the wind and trimming the sails so that they act against each other.

Heel: (vb) to lean to one side.

Jackstay: steel bar fastened to the upper side of a yard on which the head of a square sail is attached.

Jacob's ladder: ladder hung over the side of the vessel to give access to boats alongside.

Jarvis brace winch: an ingenious crank-operated mechanical device which turns yards horizontally, synchronising the movement of the two braces.

Jib-boom: spar extending the bowsprit.

Keel: the main member of a ship's structure which runs lengthwise at the bottom of the hull. 'On an even keel': with no noticeable fore-and-aft pitch, by extension with the decks practically horizontal.

Lazaret(te): store room situated in the after part of the hold.

Leech: after edge of a fore-and-aft sail or one of the vertical edges of a square sail.

Lifts: ropes running from the masthead to the yardarms. Used to adjust the vertical angle of the yards.

Line: general term for all items of cordage, chain or steel wire rope. The word 'rope' is of more restricted use.

List: (vb) to lean steadily to one side.

Lizard: a length of rope with an eye splice at one end through which a heaving line can be rove, serving the purpose of a block for light work.

Lockers: various storage compartments. Cable or chain lockers: compartments in the forepeak where the anchors' cables are stored.

Marlin spike: a metal tapered tool used for splicing rope and other sailorising jobs.

Mast: 'to serve before the mast' is to serve as a seaman, not an officer.

Nok: short metal-sheathed fixed drum fitted horizontally on the inside of the gunwale, used by the 'nokman' to stop and surge the line (nok wire) which swings a sling of cargo in or out. See Appendix 2.

Painter: mooring rope attached to the stem of a boat.

Parral or **parrel**: a collar which attaches the centre of a yard to the mast. On later square-riggers it consisted of a 'truss', a kind of metal universal joint.

Pin rail: a rack holding belaying pins, fixed to the inside of the bulwarks.

Poop: the after castle.

Pooping: a dangerous occurrence in which a vessel running before big seas is caught up and submerged by a wave coming over the poop.

Ratlines: ropes joining sets of shrouds horizontally and forming rungs for men going aloft.

Robands or rovings: short lengths of rope passed through eyelets at the head of a square sail and fastened to the jackstay.

Running rigging: lines and accessories used for raising, lowering and adjusting yards and sails.

Scuppers: openings on the side of a ship at deck level whose purpose is to carry water off the deck.

Seizing: a method of binding two ropes together or securing various items of rigging with the aid of spun yarn or wire.

Sennet or sennit: kind of flat cordage made by plaiting strands of spun yarn.

Serve: (vb) to wind a rope with small cord in order to protect it or prevent fraying.

Serving mallet: mallet with a semi-circular groove used to serve a rope tightly.

Sheer strake: the top strake.

Sheet: rope or chain fastened (a) to a lower after corner or to the boom of a fore-and-aft sail, to control its trim; (b) to both lower corners of a square sail to extend them to the yardarms below. 'To sheet home' is to trim sails to the utmost by hauling on the sheets.

Ship-rigged: with square sails on all masts.

Shrouds: ropes, forming part of the standing rigging, that steady the masts laterally.

Spurling pipe: the tube leading from the forecastle deck to the cable locker.

Standing rigging: fixed rigging used to support the masts.

Stays: ropes, forming part of the standing rigging, that steady the masts in the fore-and-aft direction (forestays, backstays). The backstays, being attached to the ship's sides, also contribute to stabilising the masts laterally.

Strake: a lengthwise row of steel plates (or planking on older vessels) in the side of a vessel.

Tack: (n) (1) lower forward corner of a fore-and-aft sail or the line controlling the lower weather corner of a close-haul square sail or staysail. (2) the direction of the ship in relation to the wind direction: 'on a starboard tack', with the wind on the starboard side.

Tack: (vb) to change tack by bringing the ship's head into the wind (as opposed to 'wearing').

Three-island vessel: a vessel with three upper decks (forecastle, centre castle, poop) separated by well decks.

Tophamper: all spars and gear above the upperdeck.

Trades: trade winds.

Trick: period of duty at a given task, especially at the wheel.

Trim: (vb) to fine-tune the bracing of the yards and the sheeting of sails in order to gain maximum advantage from the wind.

Truck: circular piece of wood at the top of a mast.

'tweendeck: a full-length deck above the lower hold. The space between this deck and the upperdeck.

Upperdeck: the highest uninterrupted deck.

Watch: a period during which a given team is on duty. The team itself.

Wear or **ware**: (vb) to change tack by bringing the ship's *stern* into the wind (as opposed to 'tacking').

Well decks: sections of the upperdeck between the castles.

Yardarms: the outer parts of a yard.

ABOUT THE AUTHOR

Max Wood was born in Dovercourt, Essex in 1930. He went to sea at sixteen years of age on a British coastal trader and retired from the sea at 63 years in Australia. Except for a stint of four years in the stevedoring industry when he worked in three of Australia's major ports, he spent his life on ships of various companies, always before the mast, under the 'Red Duster', the Australian and New Zealand ensigns, and of course the Finnish flag for two years as related in this book.

Max left British ships in New Zealand in 1952, but after a short period there went over to Australia and her ships in 1953. He subsequently involved himself deeply in the betterment of seafaring life after the 'forecastle period', and became a staunch activist of the SUA (Seamen's Union of Australia) which later amalgamated with the stevedoring workers' union into the MUA (Maritime Union of Australia).

Always eager to experience a new challenge, he has recently taken up residence in north-east Thailand following a new romance and is hoping to find the time to record more of his seafaring memories.